Gaze UPON Jesus

The beautiful color paintings on these pages are meant to be used with the reflection section "Visio Divina: Contemplate the Lord through Sacred Images" in each chapter of this book. The reflections for these images are found on the following pages:

Cavaliere d'Arpino, *Annunciation*, 1606. Photo © Vatican
Museums. All rights reserved.

Bernardino Pinturicchio, *Visitation*, ca. 1494–1496. Photo
© Vatican Museums. All rights reserved.

Giovanni di Paolo, *The Nativity*, 1440. Photo © Vatican
Museums. All rights reserved.

Raphael (Raffaello Sanzio), *Presentation in the Temple*, 1505. Photo © Vatican Museums. All rights reserved.

Federico Barocci, *Rest on the Flight to Egypt*, 1570. Photo ©
Vatican Museums.

Angelo Biancini, *Jesus in the Temple*, 1958. Photo © Vatican
Museums. All rights reserved.

"Recalling Pope Benedict's observation that an encounter with the beautiful is like the wound of an arrow that strikes our core and opens our eyes, I am confident that this volume, in its creative appeal to the heart and the imagination, will be a useful tool for opening the spiritual eyes of readers desiring to see and know the Christ child."

Most Rev. Bernard A. Hebda
Archbishop of Saint Paul and Minneapolis

"*Gaze Upon Jesus* is a unique study tool for Catholic women who long to draw close to the manger in Bethlehem and the Holy Family's home in Nazareth. With guided meditations and prayerful reflections, this book helps you encounter Jesus anew—the way Mary and Joseph did in Christ's early years."

Edward Sri
Catholic theologian, author, and speaker

"This book will be a breakthrough for many women. The beauty in this book is revealed in the unveiling of God, who is deeply personable and desires to share his very life with each of us."

Michelle Nash
President of the Military Council of Catholic Women Worldwide

"This book beautifully articulates the profound longing of the human heart: to love and be loved. Readers are led into scriptural mysteries to develop the vital art of 'gazing' through the feminine heart. I believe this work will be a healing tool in the New Evangelization, and I pray that countless women will savor it as they read. I enthusiastically recommend it."

Kathleen Beckman
Catholic author
President and cofounder of Foundation of Prayer for Priests

"This book offers fresh, insightful meditations on the earthly life of Mary that are at the same time delightful and instructive. *Gaze Upon Jesus* calls us to learn to live life in this world in a way which can lead us safely home to God in the footsteps of Mary."

Sr. Ann Shields, S.G.L.
Renewal Ministries speaker, author, and host of *Food for the Journey*

"*Gaze Upon Jesus* is one-stop shopping for the mind, the heart, and the senses for the woman who seeks to know, love, and serve Jesus in the rigors of everyday life. Through storytelling, scripture, and sacred images, it invites the modern woman to slow down in order to speed up once again to be an intentional disciple. Under the perpetual gaze of the Blessed Mother, this book gives the reader eyes to see spiritual truths and embrace the temporal world as strong Christian women modeled after Mary. It led me to a deeper communion with Christ, his Church, the saints, and my earthly family. Every Catholic woman intent on knowing Jesus should have a copy!"

Martha Reichert
President of ENDOW

"Using icons and other sacred images has always been a viable way to enhance our contemplative prayer. This book not only allows the reader to gaze upon Jesus through some beautiful *visio divina* but it also allows this gaze to be enhanced by a women's perspective. Enjoy!"

Rev. Kevin Lixey, L.C.
International Director of Patron of the Arts
Vatican Museums

"Beautifully written, rooted in the infancy narratives, and ingeniously imagined and structured, *Gaze Upon Jesus* is a marvelous encounter with the Child Jesus through feminine eyes—and the six key virtues we all can learn from it. Highly recommended."

Most Rev. Charles J. Chaput, O.F.M. Cap.
Archbishop of Philadelphia

Gaze UPON Jesus

Experiencing
Christ's Childhood
through the
Eyes of Women

Edited by **Kelly M. Wahlquist**

Founder of WINE (Women In the New Evangelization)

AVE MARIA PRESS AVE Notre Dame, Indiana

© 2019 by WINE: Women In the New Evangelization

Founded in 1865, Ave Maria Press is a ministry of the United States Province of Holy Cross.

www.avemariapress.com

Paperback: ISBN-13 978-1-59471-829-8

E-book: ISBN-13 978-1-59471-830-4

Cover images © istock.com, superstock.com, Vatican Museums.

Cover and text design by Katherine Robinson.

Printed and bound in the United States of America.

Library of Congress Cataloging-in-Publication Data is available.

Contents

Foreword
by Teresa Tomeo

I don't know too many people who are fond of long lines, of having to stand for hours in order to see something or someone. That's actually one of the reasons some avoid going to places like Rome. They can't stand the thought of fighting the crowds.

I, on the other hand, always like to see the glass as half full. Certainly, long lines aren't fun. But I look at the lines outside the Vatican Museums or St. Peter's, for example, and see a huge testimony to the glory of God. There are a lot of people of faith like you and me who travel, or hope to travel, halfway around the world to learn more about their faith and see how the great artists portrayed that faith in paintings, mosaics, and sculptures. Those same lines, no doubt, are also filled daily with art students, art history buffs, or tourists in general who are interested in the artwork and the artists. They're paying much more attention to the medium rather than the message.

And yet, no matter where they have come from and regardless of their reasons for being there, these people are gazing on the true, the beautiful, and the good. No one walks away from viewing the *Pietà* or the Sistine Chapel unaffected.

And that's my hope for you in entering into this study. Wherever you may be in your faith life, by reading this book you will be renewed and refreshed. You will see Jesus and the Church through new eyes—actually, several different sets of eyes belonging to sisters in Christ, all of whom have spent considerable time gazing at God. These sisters will help you see Jesus through their own personal experiences, through scripture, and through a famous painting or another image that illustrates our faith.

So maybe you don't know much about art and are just beginning to dive into scripture. No worries. As the great St. Teresa of Avila reminds us, "God withholds Himself from no one who perseveres."[1] The fact that you are making an effort, persevering, and taking time to go deeper is pleasing to God. While you're attempting to sharpen those gazing skills, he's been looking at you, smiling and so very pleased that in the absolute craziness of your twenty-first-century life, you're putting him front and center.

I can remember something that happened to me during eucharistic adoration not too long ago. I have a lot of trouble with distractions, which is probably one of the reasons I don't go to adoration as often as I should. But that day I made the effort to go with my husband. I brought along a new devotional given to me by a close friend whom I consider to be one of the most deeply spiritual women in my circle of friends. I sat quietly for a while, said a few prayers, and then opened the devotional. The reflection for that day nearly knocked me right out of the pew. It was words of encouragement to keep my eyes on him.

"I designed you to reflect my glory and you do so by looking to me—turning your face toward the light. The longer you stay in this light-drenched atmosphere, the more I can bless and strengthen you."[2]

Wow. I put down the book and looked back up at Jesus and just kept looking. And that's my prayer for you; that *Gaze Upon Jesus* will help you keep your eyes focused on him, "the pioneer and perfecter of our faith" (Heb 12:2).

So, consider this study your own private virtual pilgrimage to Rome or the Holy Land, minus the long lines and the hours of anticipation. The only one waiting is Jesus.

He longs to see you, and for you to see him—and yourself—more clearly. *Buon Viaggio.*

Introduction
by Kelly Wahlquist

Everyone is special on First Communion day, but I was extra special.

Now before you think I *really* lack humility, let me explain. When I was in second grade, in early September my class began preparing to receive our First Holy Communion the following April. Our planning and preparation had barely begun when Auntie Lani asked my pastor if I could make my First Communion in just a few weeks, at the Mass to celebrate my grandparents' fiftieth wedding anniversary! After many promises that my family would fully prepare me to receive Jesus in the Eucharist, it was agreed that I would make my First Holy Communion on October 18—six months before the rest of my class. I would be the only second grader who got to receive Communion every Friday at the school Mass. How could I not feel special?

My grandparents' fiftieth wedding anniversary celebration is one of the most memorable experiences of my childhood. The details are as vivid as if they happened only yesterday. Every emotion was heightened in me. I was proud to be dressed in my pretty white dress and sharing in the celebration with two people I loved deeply. I was anxious thinking about having all eyes on me, knowing I had a well-choreographed assignment of where to go and what to do. I was overjoyed to be surrounded by my entire family. And truth be told, I was super curious as to what the bread and wine would taste like. (Remember, I was only seven years old.)

The moment that I first received Jesus in Holy Communion was indeed special. My grandpa and grandma stood behind me, grandpa's right hand on my left shoulder. Then, after receiving Communion, I processed up to the left side of the altar (as Aunt Lani had told me to do) to the most beautiful statue of the Virgin Mary. As the congregation watched and the choir sang, "On This Day, O Beautiful Mother," I put a single red rose in a vase as a gift to our Blessed Mother. Then I stood nervously, wondering what I was supposed to do for the remaining three minutes and thirty seconds of the song. I anxiously fidgeted and decided I would just stand there and look at the statue until I heard the song end.

Those three minutes would change my life forever.

As I studied the woman before me, my eyes were drawn to her face. She was beautiful, and her smile was pleasant, but it was her eyes that captured me—she was gazing at me. She was looking directly at me with such a tender expression of love and compassion that I instantly felt completely at peace. The church seemed to shrink from a large building with two hundred people to an intimate space with just two. I was mesmerized by this beautiful Mother, whose gaze filled me with love. The peace I experienced was so consuming that I never heard the song end and was jarred out of the moment by the sound of my aunt's voice calling my name, as she motioned for me to take my seat.

That moment with Mary, after receiving her son, was a transforming moment for me. In her gentle gaze, my heart was opened to receive all the graces God had for me that special day and all the days to come.

There is a transforming power in the gaze of one who loves you. I experienced it that day before the statue of Mary, and I have experienced it many times since. A gaze isn't merely a look, but a look that emanates love. It is the look a mother has for her newborn baby, the look of two people falling in love, the look a father has as he walks his daughter down the aisle and gives her hand to the man who will meet her gaze for life. It is how Jesus looked at Martha as he told her she need not be anxious and troubled, and it is how Jesus looks at you. Jesus always looks at you with love. He has fixed his gaze on you. The question is, have you *fixed your gaze* on him?

Gazing upon Jesus and receiving his gaze changes our lives. It allows us to feel his deep love for us. It heals our hearts and enkindles in us a burning desire for a relationship with God. It is our hope that through the eyes of the women in this book, you will recognize and receive his gaze and be lifted up and inspired to gaze at Jesus through new eyes.

How to Use This Book

We women, by the very gifts given to us in our womanhood, see and react with our hearts. To see with the heart is to gaze. It is to look generously upon another and to see their dignity. It is to naturally want to encourage and lift up another. It enables us to live with humility and charity. It enables us to live lives of virtue.

In *Walk in Her Sandals*, we stepped into the shoes of women (factual and fictional) who were with Jesus during his Passion, Death, and Resurrection in order to more fully enter into the experience as women. In *Gaze Upon Jesus*, we will experience the Incarnation and early years of Jesus through the eyes of women (factual and fictional) who were present from the time of the announcement of the angel Gabriel until the moment the teenage Jesus was found in the temple. As we look through the eyes of women who set their gaze upon Jesus and who waited and cared for, nurtured, and encountered him, we hope to grow in virtue and holiness so that someday we will meet his gaze eternally.

This study consists of six chapters, each taking up a different vignette in the Infancy Narrative, five of which are proclaimed in the Joyful Mysteries of the Rosary. Each chapter begins with "A Moment to Ponder," which sets the stage for what will play out in each chapter.

Next, "Enter the Scripture" leads us into the scripture and unpacks the riches that are offered to us in the biblical narrative and the liturgical year. Reading the scripture citations provided beforehand makes for a powerful experience.

Following the scripture reading, a feature called "Gaze Upon Jesus" draws you deeper into the story with a fictional narrative that allows you to experience what it may have been like for women who lived and walked with Jesus. Like so many modern-day Catholic women, these ancient women were seekers and sharers of God's loving gaze.

Next, "In Search of [Virtue]" shines a spotlight on six particular virtues in such a way that you will begin to understand and live the virtues in a new and profound way—in your womanhood. I've asked Maria Morera Johnson, WINE contributor and author of two beautiful books about virtuous living, to write this part of each chapter— and I've asked her to give you here just a taste of what you can look forward to—both in her own reflections and in the fascinating fictional narrative of Stephanie Landsem.

I See You
by Maria Morera Johnson

When I was a little kid, I used to inch forward along the floor, getting closer and closer to the television screen to watch my favorite outer-space movies and television shows. My gaze would never waver, even when my mother scolded me about damaging my vision. I loved the explosions, the contours of the rocket ships, even the scary-looking aliens. I wanted to enjoy every detail.

I'm still a big fan of science fiction. Sometimes I place myself into the stories, wondering how I would react as *Star Trek*'s USS *Voyager* captain, Kathryn Janeway, or Rebel Alliance general, Princess Leia Organa, in the face of the Great Galactic War. It's probably safer to live vicariously if the annihilation of the planet is imminent.

As I've matured, special effects have taken a back seat to characterization. These modern characters fire my imagination, and while it's fun to pretend, there's more going on in the narrative. I look for characters that resonate with me and speak not only to the little girl who would scoot across the living room floor, but to the woman she has become. I look for strong female characters worthy of emulation—women who exemplify grace under fire, integrity, and intelligence while also demonstrating sensitivity and compassion.

Like St. Paul, who went into the world to evangelize, I find myself drawn to the contemporary world of entertainment as a way to discuss pertinent themes in our culture, and through those discussions, bring others closer to Christ.

The science fiction genre lends itself well to the exploration of social and religious themes because so many of the stories are otherworldly, and thus a good setting for discussing sometimes controversial themes in a nonthreatening way.

James Cameron's *Avatar* received excellent reviews from critics and fans for its beautiful special effects and was criticized for its obvious stance on US foreign policy and cultural appropriation. I, however, was immediately drawn to the way the characters address one another. A human male, Jake Sully, falls in love with Neytiri, a female inhabitant of the planet where he is sent on a mining mission. The people of this planet, the Na'vi, express their love with the phrase, "I see you."

To be seen is to be vulnerable. It is an opportunity to be fully and unconditionally loved. It reminds me of the storm of feelings and thoughts I sometimes experience in eucharistic adoration, when I gaze upon Our Lord in the Blessed Sacrament, and feel his gaze upon me.

I see you.
I acknowledge your presence.
I acknowledge your worth.
I acknowledge your uniqueness.
I acknowledge your actions and behavior.
I acknowledge the many parts of your personality that
    make you complete.
I acknowledge your faults and shortcomings.
I love you.
I love you.
I see you.

This phrase, for all its simplicity, has a depth and scope that calls to my mind the richness of the Catholic Church's teachings on the dignity of the person (see *CCC*, 1700).

Through storytelling and compelling characters, we can learn how to attain the virtues that will help us live lives of holiness. In this book, the biblical women and their accompanying fictional characters (created by Stephanie Landsem's inner gaze on biblical stories) are powerful images of holiness through virtue. We will walk with these biblical characters, not the fictional characters of popular culture who display virtue in incidental increments. These biblical women are flesh-and-blood images of virtue, which, coupled with God's grace, show us a vision of walking a woman's path to salvation under God's gaze.

The first half of each chapter opens up the scriptures and fires the imagination, helping you to truly place yourself right there with the Holy Family, and encouraging you to model the virtues of Jesus, Mary, and Joseph. In the second half of each chapter, you are guided to take what you have learned and experienced into your heart in order to apply the truths of the story to your own life, to deepen your walk with Christ.

"Reflect on the Meaning" adds a personal story from six different women today who are striving for holiness, just like you. These reflections will offer insight, encouragement, and inspiration for you on this journey.

"Visio Divina: Contemplate the Lord through Sacred Images" leads you to the next step on your journey to holiness by turning your mind and heart to the Lord in prayer. *Visio divina*, which is Latin for "divine seeing," is a method of praying with an image. *Visio divina* raises our awareness of the beauty that surrounds us and draws us deeper into the beauty of truth. As we gaze in awe upon the beautiful creations, we contemplate spiritual truths and in turn grow closer to the Creator. In his book *Meditations on Vatican Art*, Fr. Mark Haydu puts it this way: "If we learn to look with the eyes of an artist—the eyes of a prayerful wonderer—we can learn to see the love of our Creator at every turn."[1]

In this *visio divina* section, a guided reflection helps us learn to see the love of our Creator by contemplating sacred art related to the biblical narrative. You will see the image reproduced in black and white in the text of each lesson, prompting you to also turn to the full-color version at the front of the book. We suggest you take a few moments to look at the image; then read the *visio divina* text. Next, enter into prayer by meditating on the picture and contemplating the questions provided.

Since we know that as Catholics we live, and learn, and worship in community . . . and since we know that as women we are radically relational, we have added "Questions for Group Discussion." One of the best ways to use this book is in the small-group setting with other women. In fact, WINE: Women In the New Evangelization created this book and the accompanying journal for that exact purpose.[2] (If you are interested in starting a WINE book club or learning more about the WINE: Women In the New Evangelization national women's ministry, visit www. CatholicVineyard.com.)

As you read the selected scriptures, enter into the narrative, and ponder these reflections, you might find yourself asking: How am I being called to gaze upon Jesus like the women in the Bible? In what ways can I allow the gaze of Christ to penetrate my soul and transform my life? I've written a brief conclusion to each chapter, "Walking in the New Evangelization," to help you form habits that allow you to walk in virtue. This section offers two practical ways to contribute to the New Evangelization: first, by growing in your contemplative spiritual life, and second, by enhancing your active spiritual life.

This Advent, I'll be praying for you, my sister in Christ. May this book trigger a grand conversion in your heart. May these stories draw you into the early years of Jesus in a new and profound way, and may you eagerly seek and bask in the loving gaze of Christ.

1.

Gaze with Humility

(The Annunciation)

A Moment to Ponder
by Kelly Wahlquist

In the book of Isaiah, the prophet speaks to King Ahaz (735–715 BC), reassuring the king that God would not abandon his people, who were being swept up in war against two powerful enemies. Aram (Syria) and Israel would soon be destroyed, but Judah and the line of David would continue. The king hesitates, and the Lord tells the king to ask for a sign; the monarch refuses: "I will not ask, and I will not put the LORD to the test" (Is 7:12).

Isaiah's response rings down through the ages to our ears, prophesying (or heralding) a child who would one day save his people. "Therefore the Lord himself will give you a sign. Behold, a young woman shall conceive and bear a son, and shall call his name Imman'u=el" (Is 7:14).

Seven centuries pass, and now Rome is in power. In his epistle to the Galatians, St. Paul declares the freedom that rightly belongs to the children of God, who recognize in Jesus the fulfillment of God's promise of the Messiah: "When the time had fully come, God sent forth his Son, born of a woman, born under the law, to redeem those who were under the law, so that we might receive adoption" (Gal 4:4–5, RSV).

All these things—the prophets foretelling the miracle, the apostle interpreting the events of the recent past—are central to our faith. And yet, it is in the Incarnation itself—the Son of God conceived in the womb of the virgin who had with all humility fully consented to the plan of God—that is the distinctive sign of the Christian faith.

Come with me, and listen as time and space grow still, as an angel of the Lord reveals himself to a teenager from a small-town village, living in loving obscurity and poised to give assent to the plan God set in motion at the dawn of creation.

Enter the Scripture
by Sarah Christmyer

Read Luke 1:26–38 before you start.

The announcement came many months before the baby. "Aunt Sarah, guess what? We're expecting!" My niece was so excited she couldn't stop talking. "If it's a boy we have a name, but I don't know what to do if it's a girl. I wonder who he'll look like. Or she. Oh, I wonder if it will have red hair? And I can't wait to feel it move!"

It was a while before I could get a word in. Her attention was turned inside, toward the baby, and almost nothing else mattered. The eyes of her heart were busy searching the shadows of her womb, seeking any clue about who that child would be.

Today we can find out all kinds of things about a baby. Ultrasounds can tell the sex and due date, spot abnormalities, and provide a ghostly photo of the baby's face. You can test fetal DNA to find out who the father is. But no amount of scientific testing can tell you the kinds of things the angel Gabriel announced to the young girl he was sent to visit in Nazareth more than 2,000 years ago, about a child not yet conceived.

The annunciation (which is a fancy way to say "announcement") of her impending pregnancy came to Mary out of the blue. She was what we would call engaged, but more so: a binding marriage contract had been signed, and she and Joseph were considered married even though a year might pass before the wedding. In the meantime, it was customary for the girl to remain with her parents until the husband came to take her into his home. A betrothed girl who lived at home was assumed to remain a virgin.

Luke 1:26–38 gives us an intimate look at the moment Mary received the angel's message. After announcing that Jesus is coming, the same angel takes the news to Joseph after Mary conceives (see Matthew 1). However, we will focus on Luke's account as we try to see the child through Mary's eyes. A mother knows her child like no one else, and a picture starts forming for her the moment she hears about the child.

His Coming Is an Occasion of Joy

From the start, the message is suffused with joy. However irregular this birth might be, whatever clouds lie in the child's future, his coming is *good news*. "Hail, full of grace, the Lord is with you!" says the angel (Lk 1:28). The greeting comes across like a command. "Hail" is the Greek *chaire*: literally, "Rejoice!"

Mary's first impulse is not to rejoice, however. She is troubled. She turns the words over in her mind, considers "what sort of greeting this might be" (Lk 1:29). Perhaps it reminds her of similar commands in the Old Testament. Centuries before, God had sent the prophet Zephaniah to call Israel to get ready for God, who was coming to redeem them: "Sing aloud, O daughter of Zion; shout, O Israel! . . . The Lord, your God, is in your midst [literally, "in your womb"], a warrior who gives victory" (Zep 3:14, 17; see also Zechariah 9:9).

Pope Benedict XVI draws attention to "an inner resemblance between the two messages."[1] The old prophecies are coming to pass, but in a completely unexpected way. Israel had long seen God as dwelling among them as though in a womb, in the Ark of the Covenant. Now he would literally come that way. *Rejoice, the Lord is with you!* Gabriel tells Mary. "And behold, you will conceive in your womb and bear a son, and you shall call his name Jesus [God saves]" (Lk 1:31).

Clearly, God has something big in mind for her. What will it entail?

He Will Be the Promised Messiah

It has been almost six hundred years since a king sat on the throne of David in Jerusalem, and the Jews are struggling. God had promised David and his heirs an eternal kingdom; how is it that they continue to suffer under foreign rule? The verbal portrait Gabriel paints of Mary's son seems to be drawn from God's original promise to David: that his heir will be "great" and the "Son" of God; that he will sit on David's throne and his house and kingdom will be established forever. All these promises come from 2 Samuel 7 (especially verses 9, 13–14, and 16). And Gabriel's message echoes other Old Testament prophecies as well (see Isaiah 9:6, Daniel 7:14, and Micah 4:7). To any devout Jew, the picture would be unmistakable: Gabriel is describing the long-expected Messiah.

He Will Be the Son of God

This is good news, right? But Mary doesn't seem to register the picture. To bear the Messiah must have been every

Jewish girl's dream! But her mind is caught on something else: "How shall this be?" she asks. Not, "How shall this be, since I'm a nobody from nowhere," but "How can this be, since I have no husband?" (Lk 1:34).

Her confusion has nothing to do with her lowly state, or the greatness of the child. Rather, she is puzzled by the possibility of getting pregnant at all! It's only a matter of months before she is to move in with Joseph as his wife. Her question and the angel's reply provide a mind-blowing depiction of the identity of this child-to-be. The kings of Israel had long been called God's "sons" in a figurative sense. But this child will be the Son of God—literally!

We must return to the Old Testament to get the full picture. The language of God's presence and power "overshadowing" Mary comes from the end of Exodus, when God's glory overshadowed and filled the newly built tabernacle to show the people that God was living among them. Pope Benedict XVI points out that this overshadowing is "a sign of God's self-revelation in hiddenness . . . [and that] Mary appears as God's living tent, in which he chooses to dwell among men in a new way."[2]

Mary did not ask for this, nor did she expect it. It is all a work of God. And yet, the God of the Universe does not force his will upon a helpless young woman, but rather . . .

He Waits Upon Her "Yes"

The angel comes announcing, not demanding. Mary is humble; he is a gentleman. She is troubled and puzzled, yet she does not doubt. "Mary . . . carries on an inner dialogue with the Word that has been given her; she speaks to it and lets it speak to her in order to fathom its meaning," says Pope Benedict.[3] In a sense, she conceives "through her ear"—through her hearing. Her yes opens a space within, where God then makes his home. Surely God could have simply become a man. Yet the Word enters this woman and becomes flesh within her only upon her humble assent.

"I am the handmaid [Greek *doule*, "servant"] of the Lord; let it be to me according to your word," she responds (Lk 1:38). "Let it be to me." *So be it!* Hers is a perfect, joy-filled embrace of God's will and action.

When the angel leaves, Mary is left alone to ponder his announcement. But there is someone who may understand! Gabriel's parting words must have encouraged her: "And behold, your kinswoman Elizabeth in her old age has also conceived. . . . For with God nothing will be impossible" (Lk 1:36–37). Soon Mary will run to share her news with Elizabeth. I can imagine her bursting with emotion all the way there, trying to choose the right words to say. "I'm expecting . . . the messiah! Only guess what? His father is *God*!"

Prayer

Lord, help me to see Jesus. Help me to gaze at him with a humble heart, to see him as he really is. As I seek to understand what is beyond me, make your home in me.

Gaze Upon Jesus: Mary, the Mother of God
A story by Stephanie Landsem

"Mary?" My mother's voice drifted over the mist-shrouded courtyard.

"I'm here," I answered.

I stood, still and expectant, waiting for the first rays of sun to rend the eastern sky. I cherished the breaking of dawn, the threshold of a new day. When light split the horizon—fingers of gold stretching into the crimson clouds—my heart lifted in prayer. *Lord my God, your love reaches to heaven; your faithfulness to the clouds.*

The Lord was indeed faithful, for today my bridegroom would come.

Last night, Abba had drunk the cup of wine and signed the marriage contract with Joseph the carpenter. I was betrothed. The home-taking would not be for months yet—after the harvest, Abba had decided. On that day, the men of Nazareth would carry me in a litter through the streets of Nazareth. The wedding party—Joseph's friends and mine—would walk with us scattering flowers, singing, and playing their flutes and lyres. I would enter Joseph's home and become his wife.

But today, before the sun set, Joseph would come to this courtyard. We would sit together, under the watchful eyes of my parents. We would speak for the first time and he would share the evening meal with Abba. My insides fluttered like the birds rustling in the branches of the fig tree. Would he be kind? Would we be happy together? What would our lives be like?

I breathed in the scents of our small courtyard. Wisps of smoke rose from the damped cooking fire. The ancient donkey stood like a statue beside his manger, his head bowed low, his eyes closed. Shoots of herbs and onions and tendrils of cucumber vines reached for the morning sun, and flowers opened to the morning warmth. Soon, I would be a wife—with a home to care for, a husband, and children if the Lord willed it. And a garden full of flowers.

The Lord was indeed faithful.

"Mary?" the call came again. I hurried into our little clay house and found Ima rolling the sleeping mats. "There you are, my child." Her voice caught and my heart wrenched. My mother had been weeping.

I knelt down beside her and put my hands over hers. They were dry, like old parchment, and trembled. "I'll only be a short walk to the other side of Nazareth."

"I know, my daughter. Don't mind my foolish tears." Ima's smile creased her wet cheeks.

"If you had a son—" A son would not leave his parents like a daughter did.

She shushed me. "I prayed for years, my sweet daughter, and the Lord gave me my heart's desire. You." Ima brought my hands to her lips and kissed them. "A girl from the Lord's own heart."

"And he gave me the best mother in all of Nazareth . . . in all Galilee." I smiled and took the mats from her arms. "Besides, Ima, I will need to come here often to take care of the garden. My flowers will miss me."

"You and your flowers!" Ima swatted at me with a blanket. "Your husband will have to learn to eat flowers if he wants to be fed."

I laughed at the complaint I'd heard many times, glad to see her sadness lift. "Then you must come and tend my vegetables for me, Ima, or he may just starve."

She shook her head in mock disapproval. "Go now. I know you can't wait to share the news with Alda."

I put away the sleeping mats and scooped up the water jar on my way out the door. Ima was right. I couldn't wait to see my dearest friend. Alda had speculated for months on whom my father would choose for me. I suppose all the women had since I'd come of age. I couldn't wait to tell her it was Joseph.

What would she say, my dear friend who wanted only my happiness?

Would she think he was too old, or would she agree with Abba's choice for me? Her father had chosen an older man for her as well. Benjamin was a good man—although perhaps more outspoken than some thought wise. She had great respect for him and bore two children in just a few years. She could tell me what to expect.

I could hardly keep myself from running through the narrow streets.

At the well in the center of Nazareth, Alda waited her turn with a toddler clinging to her skirts and a baby tucked on her hip. She held out her free arm to embrace me.

"So, you already knew," I laughed as she pulled me close.

"Of course! News in Nazareth travels faster than a swallow in flight." She leaned back and smiled. "I wish you joy in your life with Joseph. He is a good man."

"Thank you, Alda." I said, relieved to hear her heartfelt words.

"We have much to talk about," she whispered, but her gaze fell on the other women waiting for water, "but not now."

Bilhah, the wife of the wine merchant, sidled toward me as her servant girl filled two jars at the well. "Mary," Bilhah said with a polite nod. "I, too, wish you happiness . . . and pray that your husband is not too old to give you children."

My smile faltered and my joy dimmed.

"Bilhah!" Alda spoke sharply. "Is Joseph not the most righteous man in all of Nazareth?"

Bilhah shrugged. "He may be righteous, but he is also the oldest man in Nazareth who does not have a wife. Mary could have done better to marry one of my own sons. Even my husband says it."

I hugged the cool water jar closer to my body. Could there be truth in Bilhah's words? Joseph's hair was turning to silver and his back was stooped from years bending over his work. The wife of his youth had died years ago, but he had sons—older than I, and both carpenters like their father. They had gone to Masada to find work on Herod's enormous fortress. Joseph—at his age—could leave me a widow and childless.

"I'm sure Joachim knows better for his own daughter than you or your husband, Bilhah." Alda admonished. My friend was as bold as she was loyal.

"Of course you are right, Alda," Bilhah raised her chin and looked down her nose. "At least Joseph does not think himself a prophet, telling all of Nazareth of the coming of the Messiah."

Alda winced. Her husband Benjamin did indeed believe—as did some of the rabbis—that the coming of the Promised One was nigh. He spoke of it to everyone in town, at every chance he had.

Bilhah stalked away in a huff, her servant girl laboring behind her.

I shook my head. "Don't mind Bilhah; you know how she is. As they say, 'A prophet is not without honor except in his own town.'" I held out my hands for the baby. She came to me with a gurgle and a wet smile.

Alda lowered the gourd into the depths of the well and filled her jar before speaking again. "Perhaps Benjamin is not a prophet, but I believe him." She took back the babe. "The time of our redemption is upon us; even the Pharisees say it." She called to her boy, chasing a lizard in the bushes, and leaned to kiss my cheek. "You will be happy with Joseph, and soon have a child of your own. I know it, no matter what Bilhah says."

I watched her walk away, juggling her jar, her toddler, and the babe and hoped she was right.

At home, after sharing figs and almonds with Ima, I kneeled over the grinding quern, rolling the heavy stone over handfuls of sweet grain. The thump and swoosh of the loom sounded from inside the house, where Ima worked. In the courtyard, the birds twittered and fluttered, the insects hummed, and the scent of roses drifted on the breeze.

My thoughts remained on Alda. Was it really the time of the Lord's promise—when he would send a Messiah who would lift up the poor, feed the hungry, throw the rulers from their thrones—as the prophets foretold?

The prayer of our people—the prayer on which our hope rested—filled my heart. *When, O Lord, will you send the savior to your people? When will our redeemer come?* And then another question, this one my own. *When you do send us the messiah, how will we know him, Lord?*

A soft chime, like the tinkle of silver bells, sounded over the courtyard. Strangely, it sounded like my name. I looked up, but I was alone. I went back to my grinding.

"Mary." It *was* my name, in a voice like silver. I stopped my work. The sound changed from bells to the long, low note of the shofar horn that called the faithful to worship at the Temple. "Mary." A third call. My heart sped up. What could this be?

As I made to rise, the light from the sun dimmed and what looked like a star flared in front of me, so bright I could not look at it. I covered my eyes with my hands and fell to the ground. "I am here." My words were no more than a whisper over the pounding of my heart.

The call of the horn stopped. No bird or insect buzzed. Even the sound of my own heart ceased. Was I now both deaf and blind? Was I dead? I couldn't draw a breath for the fear in my soul.

Then, the voice sounded, coming from above and below and inside me. "Rejoice, highly favored one! The Lord is with you."

The words came not in Aramaic, the language of the land, nor in Hebrew, the language of prayer—but in something else I couldn't name, yet understood. But what did such a greeting mean? Rejoice? And who was the highly favored one? Surely not me?

The presence waited.

My heart started again, thudding in my chest.

The voice came like the strumming of a lyre. I felt the chords vibrate through my body. "Do not be afraid, Mary, for you have found favor with God."

I forced my eyes to open and raised my head. I could not believe what I saw. Pure light and power stood before me. Like a man—but not a man—clothed in dazzling white. Beautiful to behold but also terrible. I dropped my gaze, fearing I would surely die. But his words—*you have found favor with God*—pierced me like a sword. This was a greeting for a chosen one . . . one such as Moses or Joshua or Jeremiah.

Not I, Lord. Surely not I? Not a girl from Nazareth.

"I come to you, Mary," the voice sang out, "for you will conceive in your womb and bear a son, and you shall call his name Jesus."

Conceive and bear a son? It seemed like time slowed, or even stopped, and yet my thoughts could not keep up. What did those words mean? How could this be happening to me? I covered my face again with my hands and bent low to the ground.

"He will be great, and will be called Son of the Most High; and the Lord God will give him the throne of his father David, and he will reign over the house of Jacob for ever . . ."

The words burned in my mind like a flame. The throne of David . . . the house of Jacob . . . Son of the Most High. These were words I knew—words of prophecy—the promises to David of the coming of the kingdom. Not words for me, a girl of lowly birth.

". . . and of his kingdom there will be no end."

And then, silence. Not the rustle of a leaf. Not the chirp of an insect. The living light waited.

The messiah . . . the Son of the Most High . . . would come. As a child, a baby . . . from me? What could I—what should I—say? My mouth was dry with fear. My whole body trembled. How would I conceive and bear a child? Now? Long before my marriage to Joseph? I did not understand, and so how could I answer? Yet who was I to question this messenger from the Lord? I must ask. I remained bowed to the ground, but I swallowed and whispered my thoughts. "How can this be, since I have no husband?"

The being came closer. Light that bright should be as hot as fire, but it did not burn. Instead it warmed me . . . calmed my spirit like a balm. "Mary."

I dared again to look up, upon the light.

"The Holy Spirit will come upon you, and the power of the Most High will overshadow you. Therefore, the child to be born will be called holy, the Son of God."

I didn't breathe. I couldn't speak. I still did not—could not—understand. It seemed impossible.

The voice continued, "And behold, your kinswoman Elizabeth in her old age has also conceived a son; and this is the sixth month for her who was called barren. For with God nothing will be impossible."

Elizabeth! For a moment, joy suffused my fear and doubt. My mother's sister was far too old to conceive. But the words of the light rang with truth.

The presence waited . . . still, expectant. Waiting for my answer.

A glimmer of knowledge filled my mind. Divine knowledge, for it was not my own. A whisper of pain worse than death, a hint of unfathomable sadness. My pain. My sadness. And then, a flash of joy so profound . . . so wondrous . . . a joy that would change not just the world . . . but eternity itself.

I could say no. I could refuse both the pain and the joy, go on with my life just like before. My parents were righteous. I was betrothed to a good man. If I said no, they would not suffer. If I said yes . . . what would Joseph do? What would my parents say?

The presence of power and light waited for my answer.

Nothing will be impossible for God. The words rang in my mind. And then I knew, I would not be alone. The Lord would be faithful. He would not abandon me—not in the joy and not in the sorrow. He would be with me. *Lord my God, your love reaches to heaven; your faithfulness to the clouds.*

I bowed down before the glorious messenger. "I am the handmaid of the Lord; let it be to me according to your word."

"Tell me exactly what the angel said." Abba's hand shook in mine.

We sat on a bench under the cedar tree, Ima on one side and Abba on the other.

I don't know how long I had lain prostrate on the ground after the magnificent light faded. I had smelled roses and dust, heard the trill of the birds and the hum of the insects. Then . . . Ima's hands lifting me, Abba's worried voice.

I took a deep breath. Abba and Ima were righteous, but would they believe me? Would anyone? How could they believe that the messiah we'd awaited would come not as a king or warrior, but as a child? A baby, born to me in Nazareth. It was too much, even for them. And Joseph, what would they tell him? What would he think of me?

I closed my eyes. *Do not be afraid. Nothing will be impossible for God.*

And so, I told them. Of the mysterious greeting, the news of a child, my question and the astonishing answer. Abba went as still as a stone. Ima's brow furrowed as she looked from me to her husband and back. I did not tell them of the pain that waited for me or the glimpse of joy. I did not tell them the child's name. I kept that in my heart.

"Do you believe me?" I said quietly. What would I do if they didn't?

Ima brought my hand to her heart.

Abba fell from the bench to his knees in front of me, kissing my hand, then bowing low to kiss my bare feet.

"Abba!" I reached down to pull him up but I stopped, knowing it was not me that he worshiped but the child I carried even now.

Ima's face was pale, her voice shook. "Of course we believe you, but . . . if you are with child . . ." she swallowed.

"She is," Abba interrupted, his head still bowed before me.

I suddenly remembered the rest of the angel's message. "And so is Elizabeth!" Ima's mouth dropped open and I rushed on. "That was the rest of what the angel said. Elizabeth is in her sixth month."

I jumped up, suddenly sure of what I must do next. Elizabeth would understand. She was the only one who could for she, too, was with child by a miracle. "I must go to her."

"To Elizabeth? But—" Ima looked from me to my father. "Surely not now?"

"Yes. Now. As soon as I can get ready." I looked to my father. "Abba, why else would the angel have told me about her?"

Abba considered, and then pulled himself slowly to his feet. "Yes," he nodded. "I will take you into the hill country. Today."

Ima stood, her hands twisting together. "But what about Joseph? He will be here, soon, and expect to find his bride. What will I tell him?"

A cold shiver of worry passed over me. We all knew what could happen if we told Joseph I was with child . . .

He could have me shamed before all of Nazareth as an adulteress. He could demand that I be stoned in front of the gate of my father's house. At the very least, he would divorce me and bring shame on Abba and Ima for the rest of their days. I looked to the sun, sinking low in the sky. This morning, I had been so certain of the life that lay before me, of God's will for me to be a wife and perhaps a mother. But now, uncertainty stretched before me like a dark night. And not just for me—for Abba and Ima and Joseph.

Do not be afraid.

I did not know what was to come, but I would not fear it. I would trust in his faithfulness, as I trusted the promise of dawn each morning.

I put my arms around Ima and for a moment, it was as if I were the mother and she the child. "Do not be afraid." I laid my cheek on her silver head. "Tell Joseph that I went to Elizabeth."

"Yes," Abba agreed. "I will send word to him that he must wait for your return. And then . . ." Abba took a deep breath.

"And then," I finished for Abba, "You will tell him the truth. And we will trust in the Lord."

In Search of Humility: The Annunciation
by Maria Morera Johnson

When the angel appeared to Mary, she received with great humility the message that she was to be the mother of God's Son. She did not run ahead of God or imagine that she had all the answers, but instead she waited on God to reveal to her his plan.

Humility is the most basic—and most needed—of all the Christian virtues, helping us to root out and to avoid pride, and compelling us to stay close to God in prayer (see CCC, 2546). It is with humility that a Christian acknowledges God as the author of all good. —Kelly Wahlquist

When my husband and I moved to a lovely bayside community in the Mobile, Alabama, area, we chose a home across the street from a quaint little church built in the 1800s. The community was founded by a family with a deep Marian devotion. Many parishioners are descendants of the family who settled here and built a chapel to recite the family Rosary.

The first time I saw the house, as we were looking at properties in the area, I heard the Angelus bells ring and knew this was the place for us. I was excited to have this physical reminder to pray. I often joked about the "smells and bells" of our Catholic tradition, and now relished the opportunity to be called to prayer!

The reality has sometimes been a bit different. At first when the Angelus bells tolled and called me to prayer, I responded promptly and wholeheartedly. But over time, the bells became part of the landscape of my life. Three times a day I hear them and sometimes muster up a Hail Mary. Then I chide myself: it wasn't supposed to be like that. I had envisioned myself being drawn to this devotion, that it would be easy—I mean, the bells are calling me!

I failed to see the obvious flaw in my plan: I had made this devotion about me. I was the starring character in a scene I created out of a Renaissance painting: the bells would toll, and I would set aside my work to pray. That didn't happen. If I was cooking, it didn't stop me. If I was mowing the lawn, I probably wouldn't even hear it. In short, I was too busy. Too proud. Too full of my own importance and the work I was doing to respond to the call.

My realization that pride was in the way of a deeper spiritual life struck me hard. I thought of the ways in which pride had stood in the way of my relationship with the Lord. Mass early on Sunday morning? Nah—there's one later. And one after that. How many long put-off opportunities for Confession?

In time I came to see how this prayer I was both drawn to and incapable of embracing wholly would help me grow closer to Mary, the Blessed Mother. In turn, Mary would gently point me to her son. It meant setting aside pride and seeking humility through prayer.

The *Catechism of the Catholic Church* clarifies the struggle I was experiencing.

> "Prayer is the raising of one's mind and heart to God or the requesting of good things from God." But when we pray, do we speak from the height of our pride and will, or "out of the depths" of a humble and contrite heart? He who humbles himself will be exalted; *humility* is the foundation of prayer. Only when we humbly acknowledge that "we do not know how to pray as we ought," are we ready to receive freely the gift of prayer. "Man is a beggar before God." (*CCC*, 2559, quoting Romans 8:26 and St. Augustine, *Sermo*)

Encouraged by scripture—"He must increase, but I must decrease" (Jn 3:30)—I asked the Lord for the grace of humility, to be able to pray as I ought, by giving myself freely to God. My *fiat* is small compared to Mary's, but it is mine—flawed as it is—and through grace and effort, and practicing humility, I endeavor to perfect it.

Consider the following as you think about the virtue of humility in your own life:

- What is an area of your life that you struggle to place in God's hands, and to give him full control? Is this something recent, or is it a chronic struggle?

- Think about the differences in how Mary and Elizabeth likely responded to the news of their pregnancies. For Mary, it was something totally unexpected, with momentous implications and even some danger. For

Elizabeth, it was a joyful recognition of something for which she and her husband had prayed for their entire married life. Which, in your opinion, required the greater humility—and why?

• While the story and even the names of Mary's parents are not found in scripture, we can imagine that it must have been very difficult indeed to hear the news of their beloved daughter's pregnancy. They were no doubt worried about the implications—what the neighbors would say, for example. How does this part of the narrative speak to you about the importance of humility in parenthood?

Reflect on the Meaning: The Annunciation
by Dr. Deborah Savage

Several years ago, as interest in St. John Paul II's writings on women was starting to gain steam, I was asked to give a talk on his signature work on this subject, his Apostolic Letter, *Mulieris Dignitatem* (*On the Dignity and Vocation of Women*, 1988) to a large gathering of young professional women. Things seemed to go smoothly until, during the Q&A period, a woman in the audience declared rather passionately that there was no way she could think of the Blessed Virgin Mary as a role model. "Mary is too passive," she said. "I have no wish to be a doormat." A number of other women nodded vigorously in silent agreement. "That's just not going to work in this day and age," someone called out. "Doormats get nowhere in a man's world," another quipped.

Their comments did not take me completely by surprise. Having worked for many years in that world, I understood, even empathized, with those women. But I also knew that their words revealed an underlying misunderstanding

about the real meaning of humility—and of who Mary actually was. And I realized that, if we were to follow John
Paul's lead, we would have to be much clearer about how
to understand the meaning of Mary's humble response to
the angel: "Let it be to me according to your word."

What does it mean to imitate Mary? The question has driv-
en me for years—and still calls to me now.

In some parts of tradition, and especially in film, Mary
has been portrayed as some naïve and clueless ingénue, a
sort of wide-eyed innocent whose understanding of what
had just happened was as mysterious to her as it was to
everyone else. I had trouble squaring this portrayal with her
given role in salvation history. She was destined to be the
Mother of God, for heaven's sake! John Paul himself points
out the incredible significance of the fact that a woman is at
the heart of salvation history. There simply had to be more
to Mary than the usual storyline.

As I investigated the text of John Paul's letter more
deeply, I found an important clue: "Through her response
of faith Mary exercises her free will and thus fully shares
with *her personal and feminine 'I'* in the event of the Incarnation" (*MD*, 4; emphasis added). My eyes widened when
I realized the profound connection the Holy Father was
signaling me with that line: unmistakable language that
communicated his own understanding of the person, which
he developed most fully in his work as the philosopher
Karol Wojtyla. Mary was the subject of her own acts, "a
conscious being, capable . . . of deciding about [her]self,
with a tendency toward self-realization."[4]

A detailed explanation of Wojtyla's account would take
us well beyond our purposes here. But there can be abso-
lutely no doubt at all that, in pointing to Mary's freedom
and her "personal and feminine 'I,'" the Holy Father was
declaring that Mary's *fiat* was an act of "radical self-deter-
mination," an essential feature of his own account of the

human person. He was casting a spotlight on the moment when the future Mother of God grasped, perhaps without fully comprehending the broader implications of the message, that her decision would determine whom she would become. And here, John Paul goes on to say, "we find ourselves, in a sense, at the culminating point, the archetype, of the personal dignity of women."[5]

The humility of Mary corresponds in every possible way to the deepest meaning of the virtue; in Mary we see humility in its supernatural setting: to be humble is to know the whole truth about myself—the gifts and the strengths, the obstacles and the weaknesses. John Paul tells us that in pronouncing herself as "the handmaid of the Lord," Mary reveals her "complete awareness of being a creature of God."[6] And here we recognize that the essential starting place of the humble is an acceptance of our status before the greatness of God, something that all of us, both men *and* women, are called to realize.

But God's action in human history has always acted through human freedom. As Fr. Benedict Ashley puts it, "Mary . . . is not a passive, submissive cipher, as sentimental piety has often portrayed her, but a figure of cosmic power."[7]

Mary's *fiat* reveals the profound significance of women; therefore, to imitate Mary in her humility most definitely does *not* mean we are to be "doormats." Mary was no doormat, no merely passive recipient of this uncommon grace. She was fully aware of herself and, though she cannot have known in any complete sense the significance and specific meaning of her yes to the angel, she nonetheless made the decision to say yes freely—and with full recognition of her freedom to do so.

St. John Paul tells us that Mary is *the* model and prototype, indeed the epitome, of the feminine genius. If that is the case, then we *should* find in Mary the clue as to how to manifest that in fulfilling our mission. What does it mean to imitate the genius of Mary? Does it mean I am to appear to float serenely through life, as if on a cloud? Certainly not. So what sort of model does Mary represent "on the ground"?

Clearly, we need a proper, more realistic account of the personhood of Mary.

We discover our first clues in Luke's account of the Annunciation (see Luke 1:26–34). Luke describes a self-possessed young woman who is anything *but* a clueless, giddy teenager. When Mary is approached by the angel, Luke tells us that she "was greatly troubled" by his words and asked herself "what sort of greeting this might be." She doesn't cower or take flight or panic. She *pauses* and she *thinks*; she first asks *herself* a question: What could these words mean? (see Luke 1:29). St. John Paul II tells us, "She is in a state of complete, personal recollection."[8]

And what is Mary's response when the angel declares that she will conceive and bear a son? She does not giggle or blush. She asks another intelligent question, a woman's question: "How can this be, since I have no husband?" (Lk 1:34). It is really the equivalent of saying, *Hey, wait a minute here—I know how these things work. And you are going to have to explain this to me a bit.*

Truly, who among us would have the presence of mind to respond to such an announcement from an *angel* who suddenly appeared on our doorstep with such an obvious and common-sense question? I lose my cool waiting in traffic!

No—Mary was no ordinary woman. She was a self-possessed, fully collected young woman who asked some very intelligent and sensible questions upon hearing that she was to be the Mother of God. And this makes some sense when we consider what we know already about who Mary is. Indeed, who was Mary?

A moment's reflection will remind us that, according to our faith, she was conceived *without* sin, completely free of the effects of the Fall. If that is the case, we certainly must ask a further question: What sort of self-knowledge would she possess? There can be no doubt that it would have been profoundly complete, at least for her age and development level. Mary would have to have been in full possession of herself and, however unexpected, prepared by the stability of her personhood, to receive the message of the angel.

When Mary utters her *fiat*—"let it be to me according to your word" (Lk 1:38)—she most definitely *is not* the unsophisticated, wide-eyed maiden usually portrayed in movies. Scripture, tradition, and the work of St. John Paul II together reveal that Mary's *fiat* was a radical act of human freedom in which she participated fully—and thus changed the course of human history. No doormats here.

This is the commission given to woman—to us. It is to the fullness of what it means to be a woman that the Church calls us. As Pope Pius XII told the women of his day: "It is not enough to be good, tender, generous; one must also be wise and strong."[9] And in Mary we see a model of what that means. We are to bring not only our natural capacity to attend to the needs of others to the tasks of human living; we must also offer our wisdom, our strength, our love, indeed *everything we are* to that mission.

To choose Mary as a model for our own lives is to be women of cosmic significance—who say "Yes!" to God without fear or refusal—in an act of authentic human freedom.

In his letter to the Romans, St. Paul wrote, "If, because of one man's trespass, death reigned through that one man, much more will those who receive the abundance of grace and the free gift of righteousness reign in life through the one man Jesus Christ" (5:17).

By divine provision, Mary was the first to experience this infusion of "abundance of grace" from the moment of her conception and was perfectly free to give herself wholeheartedly to the will of God. In so doing, she became through her obedience everything that Eve—mother of us all—was not: a singular example of a heart surrendered out of love for God.

While we do not know that she was able to anticipate every hardship and obstacle her yes would entail, we can be confident that she was an intelligent young woman who knew that these hardships would come. And yet, she said yes just the same. How is God calling you, today, to give that hard yes over to him, thereby imitating Mary not only in her intelligence but also in her surrendered heart? —Kelly Wahlquist

Visio Divina: Contemplate the Lord through Sacred Images

by Dr. Elizabeth Lev and Kelly Wahlquist

Cavaliere d'Arpino, *Annunciation*, 1606. Photo © Vatican Museums. All rights reserved.

The ancient spiritual practice of visio divina *invites the faithful to contemplate the Lord, as St. Paul said, "with the eyes of the heart" (Eph 1:18). In his book* Transformed by God's Word, *Stephen Binz points out that* visio divina, *like lectio divina, "[invites] us to both listen and see deeply . . . to make us present to the saving event."*[10]

As we contemplate the use of light and color, the imagery and symbolism, and the appearance of the figures within each image, we are drawn deeper and deeper into prayer.

The image for this *visio divina* exercise is *Annunciation* by Cavaliere d'Arpino (1606). The original hangs in the Vatican Museums' Pinacoteca (Painting Gallery) in Rome.

Born and raised in Rome during the era of the Catholic Restoration, the talented Giuseppe Cesari, later known as Cavaliere d'Arpino, designed the mosaics for St. Peter's dome, painted the august hall of the Capitoline Palace, and worked on other important projects in the last years of the sixteenth century. He also painted works on canvas, one of which is *Annunciation*.

Find the color image of d'Arpino's *Annunciation* at the front of the book. Spend a few moments gazing on it before returning to the reflection. Use a bookmark to hold your place so you can return to it easily.

Focus your heart and your attention on the characters in the painting, noticing their expressions and movements as well as the colors, spaces, and shapes that surround them. Ask the Holy Spirit to help you look with the eyes of a prayerful wonderer and contemplate what you see.

Against a dark, stoic background, the warm tones of Mary's gown, the angel's robe, and the golden glow of the dove (Holy Spirit) propel to the forefront the story of the Annunciation, the moment in salvation history when heaven and earth stood still, awaiting the young virgin's response to the angel—the moment we are first told of the Incarnation, the Word made flesh.

Notice the setting that gives way to the warmth of the moment. Artists choose different moments of the Annunciation to depict. In this image, our attention is focused on the pondering of Mary at the angel's strange greeting.

The stone backdrop, the steps leading to an open area, and the wooded lectern upon which Mary is leaning resemble a church. Stark architectural confines are indicative of the attempt to make order in one's life, yet this sober space also draws the eye to the softness of the encounter.

Place yourself in the scene. Imagine you are Mary, head bowed in gentle humility, heart contemplating the words of the angel, arms open to the will of God. Stay in that moment, meditate on the Annunciation, and reflect upon your own life. What area of your life needs order? Do you feel God is calling you to give your yes to something you can't completely comprehend? Ask Mary to help you follow in her footsteps and to respond to God's will with a humble and trusting heart.

Questions for Group Discussion
by Dr. Carol Younger

The essence of WINE is to bring women into relationship—relationship with one another and into an intimate relationship with the Lord. One way to do this is in the small group setting. Below are questions relating to various sections of the chapter to help each member of the small group grow in knowledge and faith. As trust and sharing increase, relationships flourish and friendships are made. For tips on how to run a fruitful small group, visit CatholicVineyard.com. —Kelly Wahlquist

1. Mary is your smartest and dearest friend. Today, her eyes are shining; she smiles as she takes both your

hands, looks directly in your eyes. She wants to tell you
the most amazing things about *your share* in *her joy* and
the plans of the Lord. What does she say to you? What
is your response to Mary's invitation?

2. Mary's response to the angel is "Let it be to me." What
is your mission in the Incarnation, in bringing Jesus to
the world? Knowing he's coming in a Second Advent,
what can you do to prepare for that moment? Will you
pray differently now? Will you teach someone about
him soon? How will you share your joy and faith in him
in a new and inviting way?

3. Beginning the Joyful Mysteries, Mary reflects on the
meaning of her day, just before archangel Gabriel
arrives. She thinks, "Soon my bridegroom will come."
Each time you go to Mass, you go in anticipation of
uniting with your Bridegroom in Holy Communion.
Do you anticipate him with Mary's joy? How do you
prepare to meet him?

4. After the annunciation and her *fiat*, Mary trusts herself
and her whole future, temporal and eternal, unafraid
that she would—someday—understand the Lord's
working in her life. What aspect of your life needs an
internal act of trust in the Lord Jesus at this moment?

Walking in the New Evangelization
by Kelly Wahlquist

As we conclude this chapter, think about how each aspect
has spoken to your heart. What have the scriptures revealed
to you? Which qualities of the women in the story resonated
with you? How have your eyes been opened to walking in

humility? Here are a couple of ways you can continue to reflect upon what you have discovered and grow in virtue.

Virtue in Action

A beautiful way to humble your heart and grow in humility can be carried out as you prepare to meet Jesus, your Bridegroom, at Mass. At the moment of consecration, as the priest raises the consecrated host (and then the chalice that holds the Precious Blood), in your heart say, *My Lord and my God.* As the priest then genuflects after the elevation of host and the elevation of the chalice, in your heart pray, *Jesus Christ, Son of the Living God, have mercy on me, a sinner.*

Another prayer that helps me grow in humility is one I learned from my pastor, Fr. Steve. It is one I find myself praying when life seems overwhelming. Simple and to the point, it keeps me humble and reminds me daily how much I need him: *You are God and I am not.*

Until next time, ask God for the courage and insight to recognize the opportunities that God sends to us to say yes and to grow in humility and faith.

2.

Gaze with Patience

(The Visitation)

A Moment to Ponder
by Kelly Wahlquist

In our increasingly mobile society, it can be hard to find lasting friendship, bonds that can be measured in generations. Growing up, my friends' grandparents were like extended family. My friend Molly's grandma was always Grandma Esther to me. Our children experience that dynamic today with our friends in New York, whom they know as "Uncle Bob" and "Aunt Judy" even though we share no biological tie.

It was this prolonged familiarity that made me feel safe turning to Grandma Esther as I was growing up, and it is that same commitment and familiarity my children now experience with their East Coast aunt and uncle; they have a safe place to turn in the adversities of life. Can you think of people who played this kind of role in your life?

Loyalty. Longevity. Reliability. These are the characteristics of the kind of lasting friendship that the book of Sirach describes, a kind of natural grace that provides much-needed support in both happy and troubled times:

Faithful friends are a sturdy shelter:
 whoever finds one has found a treasure.
Faithful friends are beyond price;
 no amount can balance their worth.
Faithful friends are life-saving medicine;
 and those who fear the Lord will find them.
Those who fear the Lord direct their friendship aright,
 for as they are, so are their neighbors also. (Sir 6:14–17,
 NRSV)

In this chapter on the Visitation, we catch a glimpse into the inner life of both Mary and Elizabeth. They were kinswomen separated by both distance and age. And yet, when Mary hears the words of the angel, her first thought is to fly to this older woman, to find in her a safe place, a place that would lessen her sorrows and double her joys. Elizabeth, whose long-suffering patience had at last been rewarded with new life, would listen to Mary with equal patience and help her to process what she could barely understand herself.

Yes, faithful friends are all the things Sirach said: a sturdy shelter, a treasure, beyond price, life-saving medicine. As you continue to gaze at Jesus through the eyes of the delighted Elizabeth, may you see for yourself the goodness of offering yourself in joyful, faithful, lifelong friendship to a soul that needs what you have to offer.

Enter the Scripture
by Sarah Christmyer

Read Luke 1:39–45 before you start.

It takes three or four days to walk the eighty miles from Nazareth, where Mary lived, to the Judean hill country and the home of her relatives Elizabeth and Zechariah. Today you can stand on the terrace in front of the Church of the

Visitation in Ein Kerem and look out over those hills, imagining the young and newly pregnant Mary making her way there. She may have gone "with haste" (Lk 1:39), but she had plenty of time to reflect on the miracle that was beginning inside her.

Maybe the angel's words, that Elizabeth had conceived in her old age for "with God nothing will be impossible" (Lk 1:36–37), reminded Mary of the child God promised to Abraham and Sarah in their old age, saying, "Is anything too hard for the LORD?" (Gn 18:14).

She may have recalled other times in Israel's history when God made a barren woman fruitful and gave her child a special role in his plan: not just Abraham and Sarah's son Isaac but also Jacob, Samson, and Samuel.[1] Maybe she remembered Hannah, the mother of Samuel, who burst into praise when she conceived against hope (see 1 Samuel 2:1–10). Was Mary's mind filled with that song as she anticipated meeting the elderly Elizabeth, who was six months into her own impossible pregnancy? Without a doubt—God was doing something great!

The greatest thing of all—God's arrival as a human being—came slowly, gently. His presence is manifested first in his effect on others, as a stone dropped into a pond is known by the ripples it makes:

The First Ripple: His Word Brings Life

It all starts with the Word of the Lord, *the Word* himself going out as a spoken word conveyed by the angel. The message reaches Mary's ears, prompting her to give her *fiat*. And with that humble surrender, she receives God's life within her.

The Second Ripple: His Approach Brings Joy

Mary flies to Elizabeth, who has been uniquely prepared to welcome her.

John leaps for joy in his mother's womb on hearing Mary's greeting. The first recognition of the Word made flesh comes in the joyful embrace of two faithful women and their unborn children.

The Third Ripple: His Presence Prompts Understanding and Rejoicing

Elizabeth is filled with the Holy Spirit. As a result, she recognizes the unique blessedness of Mary as mother of Jesus and as the model disciple who believes and accepts the transforming power of the Word of the Lord (see Luke 11:28).

The Fourth Ripple: His Existence Manifests the Father

Mary erupts into praise of God's mercy and triumphant glory, the proof of which is taking shape within her womb. At that moment he is just a tiny speck tossed into a small, hidden, back corner of the world; yet the ripples will go out into the sea of humanity until they fill the earth, the fulfillment of God's promises in a new and perfect covenant.

The Ark of the New Covenant

The astute reader will notice in Elizabeth's Spirit-inspired proclamation allusions to the Old Testament description of a high point in Israel's history: when David, having been made king over all Israel, established his throne in Jerusalem and sought to take there the Ark of the Covenant—the earthly "throne" of God's presence among them (see 2 Samuel 6). Here we see several parallels:

- David asks, "How can the ark of the LORD come to me?" (2 Sm 6:9)—as Elizabeth asks, "And why is this granted me, that the mother of my Lord should come to me?" (Lk 1:43).

- In 2 Samuel 6:11, we read that "the ark of the Lord remained in the house of O'bed-e'dom . . . three months"—as Mary "remained with [Elizabeth] about three months" (Lk 1:56).

- And David danced with joy before the ark (see 2 Samuel 6:14) even as John leapt in his mother's womb at the approach of Mary (see Luke 1:44).

By borrowing this language from scripture, Luke shows us that what was from the start a distinguishing feature of God's people—his presence among them in the Ark of the Covenant—was only a hint of the far more marvelous truth. Mary is a "new Ark" through which not only God's glorious present but also God himself in the flesh comes to live in and with his people!

There is another verbal clue that points to Mary as the new Ark, and that is Elizabeth's joyous exclamation on her approach (see Luke 1:42). Luke uses the Greek *anaphoneo*, which means "to cry out with a loud voice, exclaim." This verb is used nowhere else in the New Testament, and in the Greek Old Testament, it's used only for joyous shouting and music before the Ark of the Covenant.[2] This very special type of praise is also fitting at the approach of the one who bears the very presence of God, made flesh in her womb.

God is truly present in Mary! No wonder she herself breaks out in praise. In Mary's song, which we know as the Magnificat, after the Latin translation of its first line (*Magnificat anima mea Dominum*, "My soul magnifies the Lord"), she draws on a long line of biblical songs of women.[3] She has learned these songs through years of meditating on scripture and learning by heart the Word that is now taking flesh in her. Now this flowers forth in a song that gives those old songs their true meaning. The great things that God has done throughout history—showing strength and mercy and fulfilling his promises—all are about to take definitive shape in the fruit of Mary's womb.

I suppose God could have dropped onto Earth fully grown, as a man. And yet he entrusts himself to others and to the hidden necessity of waiting. That will require patience on Mary's part, as it has for Israel these generations. But as he has done with Mary—regarding her "low estate" and doing "great things" for her (Lk 1:48–49)—he has done for Abraham and will do "to his posterity for ever" (Lk 1:55).

Prayer

Lord, help me see Jesus! As he entrusts himself to others and to me, help me gaze in patient joy and expectation as I await the fulfillment of your promises.

Gaze Upon Jesus: Elizabeth, the Kinswoman of Mary

A story by Stephanie Landsem

I had avoided the well for months. Indeed, I had hardly left the house since I realized what was happening to me.

Perhaps I was afraid this bewildering blessing would end in sorrow, or perhaps it was the reaction of the other women I feared. Whatever the cause, I reached my sixth month and ended my seclusion. I went that morning to the well in the center of town, my water jar bumping against my swelling belly and my heart thumping in my chest. Would the women be shocked that at my age I had conceived a child? Would they wonder—as I did—if I could bear a child or, indeed, live long enough to see it raised?

At least ten women stood at the well, clustered like hens as they shared the village news or bent over their water jars. Their talk died away as I approached. I set my jar on the stone ledge and straightened to see every eye on my burgeoning middle, every mouth gaping. As one, they looked to my face, and then to each other, brows raised high and eyes wide as if to say, *Could it be?*

I needn't have worried. Despite my age, perhaps even because of it, their joy was great.

"The Lord has shown great mercy to you, Elizabeth!" And indeed he had.

"Blessed are you and your husband!" And so we were.

Miriam, my maidservant, stood in line to fill our water jars as each woman in turn came to offer her good wishes. Some were friends, who embraced me. Others were hardly known to me. All were amazed.

In truth, I could still hardly believe it myself.

My hair had turned to silver and my breasts sagged. My joints creaked and groaned in the morning. And yet new life grew within me. I was joyful, of course, and full of praise for the Lord. For the way in which this marvel came about was as astonishing as the miracle itself.

For years, the women of our town had not hidden their pity toward me and my barren womb, shaking their heads and clucking their tongues. "A large house and so many servants, but no child." The men wondered at my husband, Zechariah, saying, "He would be within the law to put her aside."

My trust is in the Lord, I prayed each month. *I will wait on his faithfulness.*

Of course, Zechariah did not put me aside, for he was a righteous man. In our youth, Zechariah had been as eager as any young man who wished for children. But as years passed, his hope for children dimmed and so did his ardor. Our home remained empty, and to my sorrow, Zechariah became a stranger to my bed.

And yet, as the years settled upon us, the Lord blessed our marriage in other ways. Zechariah asked my counsel in his dealings with merchants and traders. He gave me a free hand in the running of the household. I fed the poor who begged at my gate and took in those who needed work. I had loyal servants, trusted stewards, and a husband who respected me. What right had I to grumble? And so, when my heart ached for a tender touch from my husband, I reminded myself that I was a fortunate woman. And when I yearned for Zechariah's embrace—for him to take me to his heart—I told myself to be grateful.

My trust is in the Lord, I continued to pray. *I will wait on his faithfulness.*

Then—six months ago—Zechariah went to Jerusalem. And when he came back . . . blessed, indeed. Amazed. Dumbfounded.

Miriam filled the second jar, and the matrons finally turned their attention from me to speak of the unrest that seethed from Galilee to Jericho.

"How long must we wait on the Lord's promised one?" Devorah said. Her robe was tattered and her cheeks gaunt. "Herod's taxes have taken all I have."

"Perhaps Herod himself is our savior," Tzillah countered. The wine merchant's wife was rosy and well fed. "He's rebuilt the Temple and kept the peace with the Romans."

I took the first filled jar from Miriam and hefted it on my hip. I had no desire to enter into argument with Tzillah—but truly, Herod the savior? Ridiculous.

Devorah stepped up to Tzillah, a challenge in her voice. "A friend to Herod is no friend of mine. And any who desire peace with Caesar is indeed the enemy of Judea."

Tzillah looked down her nose at Devorah. "Enemies of Rome get crucified. Enemies of Herod lose their heads."

Miriam and I left the women to their bickering. Nothing had changed from when I last came to the well. Here, only a half-day's journey from Jerusalem, women felt the pressure of the coming storm. The rabbis and scribes talked of the coming of the kingdom while desperate men joined bands of rebels and Roman troops patrolled the countryside like dogs in search of scraps of meat. Some looked for the messiah in every stranger's face. I doubted the Lord would send the savior to this little town in the hill country.

No, Herod was not our savior, and Caesar would not bring peace. The Lord had promised his people a messiah who was both just and merciful; these men were neither. Walking home, I lifted my heart in prayer. *When, O Lord, will you send the savior to your people? And how will we know him, when he comes?* Would he come as a king, like Herod? Or with a conquering army, as Caesar had done? Only the Lord knew.

At the home I shared with Zechariah, near the city walls but away from the bustle of the marketplace, I labored at the tasks of my station. Miriam swept the sleeping rooms while I polished the ebony dining couches and repaired one of the silk cushions. I directed two servants—brothers with bright smiles but easily distracted minds—to their labor in the garden, then set another—a grizzled man who had come as a beggar and stayed as a servant—to butchering a goat for our evening meal. After sending Miriam to the market with a warning not to pay too much to the grain merchant, I helped my silent husband with his accounts until the sun began to sink in the western sky.

Finally, I walked through the arched doors into the cool of the courtyard. My back throbbed and my spirit flagged. I would take a rest—just a short one—before the preparations for the evening meal. The shade beneath the pomegranate trees and date palms was fragrant with lilies and roses. I settled on a bench beside a burbling marble fountain and was about to close my eyes when my steward approached, his mouth pinched.

"What is it?" I rubbed my aching back.

"A man and girl at the gate. They look like beggars."

I let out a short sigh. Rest would come later. "Bring them to me." Our home was known as one of charity in these times when charity was in short supply. "Miriam, bring bread and some of the smoked fish."

I prepared a smile and kind words. My steward returned not with strangers, but my sister's husband, Joachim. He looked worn and worried. Concern sprung to my mind—could Anne be unwell? I stood; then I saw that behind my brother-in-law was—

"Elizabeth!" Mary's voice rang out and suddenly . . . a kick within my womb—a kick such as I had never felt before!—bent me double.

"Mary!" I gasped. My hands flew to my belly where I could feel the child roll and push. But it was not only the surprise of pressure on muscle and skin; it was something else—a rush of joy far exceeding my fondness for Mary. A burst of revelation like a fire ignited in my heart. I opened my mouth and words poured from it that were not my own. They came from the joy, from the burning fire.

"Most blessed are you among women, and blessed is the fruit of your womb!"

The steward gasped. Of course, he wondered why I, a woman of stature, would greet a girl like this. But I didn't care for custom. I could only marvel at the knowledge that flamed within me.

I stumbled toward Mary, still holding my hand over the child who was dancing in my womb. "And why is this granted me, that the mother of my Lord should come to me?" I grasped her outstretched hands in mine, the words of the Spirit pouring from me like water from a fountain. "Blessed are you . . . Blessed! You, Mary, believed that what was spoken to you by the Lord would be fulfilled."

Mary's face lit up in understanding. She pulled me close. "Elizabeth," she drew my hand over her belly, the secret so small, but we both knew what was there. "My soul magnifies the Lord."

Tears welled in my eyes and I brought Mary's hands to my face, kissing them.

"My spirit rejoices in God, my Savior, for he has regarded the low estate of his handmaiden." Her eyes shone with tears. "For behold, henceforth all generations will call me blessed."

Again the child in my womb leaped for joy between us. Mary, this girl—this woman—had been chosen by God. I knew that as surely as that the sun rose in the east. She was the one to bring the Lord's promise to his people. As a baby! A child in the womb!

And—in some mysterious way—I knew that the Lord had given this knowledge to my unborn child, and passed it to me even as I heard her greeting. *How wonderful, my Lord, are your works!*

"Go quickly," I told the gaping steward, my heart still pounding with joy. "Get your master, Zechariah. We must hear what the Lord has done."

Zechariah and I listened to Mary's story in amazement. Joachim sat beside her, holding her hand as she told us the angel's words. A child, born of the Spirit, was destined to save his people. I marveled at the story and knew its truth in my heart. Zechariah nodded vehemently at her description of the Lord's messenger.

"You have seen him too?" Mary asked. "The angel of the Lord?"

Zechariah bent his head, tears brimming in his eyes, his bony hand clutching mine.

Indeed, from this day forward all generations would call this humble maid blessed. I spoke the words I could only imagine were on my husband's heart, since he could not say them for himself. "Your child—the Son of the Most High—and ours. Both heralded by an angel." I put a hand over my own womb. "What does it mean?"

Zechariah motioned for his writing tablet and scribbled on the wax with the stylus before handing it to Joachim and pointing to my rounded belly.

"He will be filled with the Spirit, even from his mother's womb," Joachim read, "and will prepare a people fit for the Lord." Joachim looked up in surprise. "An angel told you this?"

My husband nodded. I felt tears prick my eyes, and he put his arms around me, pulling me close.

A son. Our son. Filled with the Spirit. He would prepare the way for the Messiah.

I pressed my face close to my husband's heart, filled with an ache of joy mingled with fear. The messiah would bring down the mighty from their thrones. Herod. Caesar. They would not fall without the shedding of blood.

Whose blood would it be?

My trust is in the Lord. I reminded myself again.

The chill of night crept into the courtyard, and the insects began their song. We left the men with another cup of wine and brought Mary's few belongings into my best sleeping room. Brass lamps chased away the dark, and a brazier glowed in the corner. The mattress was filled with sweet-smelling straw and covered with the finest linen. I pulled back the wool blankets and embroidered coverlets for my tired niece.

"Tell me what happened to Zechariah," she said.

I sat down heavily beside Mary on the plump mattress. How could I tell her what had happened when I hardly understood it myself? For the last twenty-five years I'd lived with Zechariah. I knew his ways as I knew my own; sometimes it seemed I knew his very thoughts. He was a good man—a righteous man—but not a surprising one. Until the day he returned from Jerusalem . . .

"When he last visited the Temple," I began as I pulled the covers over her as if she were a child, "they told me he was chosen to enter the sanctuary to burn the incense. He was inside for a long time, long enough that people started to talk. And when he came out," I waved toward the outer courtyard, "he was like that."

Mute. Not a word or sound left his mouth. But he was changed in more than that way. Mary waited for me to go on.

"He came home. And when he walked through the gate, there was a look in his eyes . . ." I felt my cheeks warm. I hadn't seen that look for many years.

"What?" Mary asked, her voice puzzled. She was still a maiden, after all.

"He walked across the courtyard and . . . and he kissed me in front of all the servants!"

Astonishing. Unbelievable.

From that day forward, he was like the bridegroom of our youth. He bade me to sit with him at dinner and poured my wine. He held my hand when we walked together. Even more astounding, he was like a young man in the night, coming to my bed and kissing me sweetly. I didn't need to tell Mary the rest, but I feared my girlish blush belied the unspoken words.

And then, the impossible happened. "When I told Zechariah I was with child, he knelt before me and wept."

Mary wrapped her warm hands around mine. "What can it all mean?" she whispered. Her question echoed through the dark night and joined my own.

What, indeed, could it all mean?

I returned to the courtyard where Joachim and Zechariah stared at the embers of the dying fire. "Stay with us," I said, and Zechariah nodded his agreement. "For as long as you wish."

Joachim rubbed his face and shook his head. "I must leave tomorrow. Anne will be worrying, and we have yet to tell Joseph."

"What will he do?" I asked. Zechariah covered my hand with his and we exchanged anxious looks. We knew the law and what could happen to Mary.

Joachim let out a long breath. "I don't know." I could hear the worry in his voice. "Joseph is a righteous man but this—" he waved to the house where Mary slept. "I truly don't know."

My prayer whispered again in my heart. *Remember his faithfulness.*

Three days later, a man appeared at our gate with weathered skin and travel-dusted cloak. I was not surprised, for I had been expecting him.

Zechariah and I had deliberated in the one-sided way we had learned to speak. If Joseph was merciful, he would divorce Mary quietly. But when her pregnancy began to show, everyone in Nazareth would know his shame. He would be humiliated, and many would call him weak. Mary would have to leave Nazareth and raise her child—somehow—alone.

Unacceptable.

If, though, Joseph valued justice over mercy, he could denounce her publicly. He would be considered a righteous man, one who followed the law, but Mary would bear the full brunt of his justice . . . she could be stoned.

Unthinkable.

Joseph met my gaze, and I wondered if mercy or judgment lay behind those tired eyes.

Mary smoothed her robe and pulled her headscarf into place as she followed me to Zechariah's study. Joseph sat in a carved chair with a woolen cushion. A cup of wine and tray of bread and dried figs sat untouched at his elbow. Zechariah stood silently at the large window that let in the afternoon light. The servant girl finished washing Joseph's feet with jasmine-scented water and hurried out of the room.

Mary stood before her betrothed, her head bowed in respect. I was struck by her peace. She was not afraid of this man who could shame her, even have her killed.

Joseph looked at Mary for a long moment with an expression I didn't understand. "Mary," he began, his voice low as if he spoke only to her. "I thought many things on my journey here. Many things." He shook his head. "That you had betrayed me. Shamed yourself." He ran a hand over his face. "I agonized over the story your father told. I didn't want to believe it, but I also knew that Joachim would not lie to me."

Joseph's face was creased with confusion, but I saw no anger. Not yet.

He stood, paced across the room, and then came back to Mary. "I fought myself with every step toward you. Crying out to God. Asking for his guidance."

Mary raised her eyes to his, still calm as a placid lake. I marveled at her courage.

Joseph swallowed hard. "I desire to do right, Mary. Toward you and the law."

My heart pounded, and I glanced at Zechariah. His eyes were fixed on Joseph. Would Mary's betrothed demand she return with him to Nazareth, to face her punishment?

Joseph continued as if it were only Mary and him in the room. "I planned to divorce you," he said, and then quickly added, "quietly, I decided, after my anger cooled. You are young and I am . . ." He shook his head. "But then," his voice dropped, "while I slept in the wilderness, the second night of my journey, I had a dream. Not really a dream . . . a messenger from God."

Zechariah straightened and drew a sharp breath.

"I don't understand it," Joseph reached out, as if imploring Mary to help him understand. "But I believe it. He told me that you, Mary . . . you carry the child of the Most High."

He knew? My breath caught in my throat.

And then Joseph bowed down before Mary, the woman he had every reason to believe had betrayed him. Zechariah clutched at my hand, his gaze on the man and women before us.

Joseph continued, his voice sure. "You, Mary, will be my wife, and I will be your husband. And this child—this son . . . I will treat him as my own."

I let out my breath. Unbelievable. The Lord had worked his plan long before the angel had spoken to Mary. He had brought to her a husband close to his own heart—a man of both justice and mercy, of humility and righteousness.

Zechariah snatched a tablet from his desk and wrote, then thrust it to me.

I glanced at my husband in question, but he motioned to Joseph impatiently. "Did the messenger tell you what you are to name the child?" I related.

Joseph's brow furrowed. "Yes, he told me the child's name."

Mary finally spoke. "I, too, was told the name." She smiled as if they shared a secret, for indeed they did—the name of the unborn child. "Jesus." Mary said, "his name shall be Jesus."

Joseph's face lit with wonder. "Yes. That is what the messenger said. Jesus." He reached for Mary's hands and grasped them in his own. "God is with us."

The child in my womb once again let loose with a mighty kick. Zechariah turned to me and pulled me into his arms, embracing me with a strength I didn't know he possessed. My heart sang as our son danced within me.

The Lord had sent the Promised One. As a baby, a child of Mary. And he had provided a merciful and just man to watch over them both.

The Lord God was with us. Indeed, he was with us even now.

In Search of Patience: The Visitation
by Maria Morera Johnson

"Love is patient and kind" (1 Cor 13:4). The Catechism tells us that patience is one of the twelve fruits of the Spirit, "perfections that the Holy Spirit forms in us as the first fruits of eternal glory" (CCC, 1832). Over time, the tiny seeds of virtue grow, often through testing. He forms in us perfect patience through waiting on his perfect time. This is something Elizabeth and her husband understood as they waited for God to bless them with children. And Mary's pregnancy, too, gave her family and Joseph an opportunity to wait upon the Lord, trusting him to reveal the next step, and the next, in his plan for them. While some of us have to work harder than others to grow in this particular virtue, on a natural level, we can be sure that when we are being tested, the supernatural graces are there for the asking! Listen as Maria recounts her own experience. —Kelly Wahlquist

People who've seen me teaching compliment me for having a lot of patience with my students. I don't often agree with that—perhaps I am merely demonstrating a professional demeanor that I have practiced for decades, but I don't readily think of it as patience. I'm inclined to think of patience in relationship to its flipside, impatience. I lean toward impatience. I want things immediately. Long lines exasperate me. I just don't like the idea of waiting and often catch myself sighing dramatically and even complaining aloud. Regrettably, more often than not I fall into the whiny "but I want it now" habit, and it clouds my mood and no doubt sets a bad tone for others around me. I don't like this about myself, and I pray for the grace of patience.

You know how that goes. The Lord gives me ample opportunities to practice this virtue. At the store. In the bank. With the dog. Delays make me crazy.

Patience, however, tolerates difficulties and delays. The patient person responds with calm to things that cannot be controlled. The patient person waits. And waits. And often waits some more.

Like the other virtues, patience can be developed. We can train ourselves to respond to the irritation in our lives with calm, and we can learn to treat these incidents as opportunities for moral growth. In this way, maybe I have been exhibiting patience with my students by responding with love and calmness. Exercising self-control to keep from rolling my eyes and refraining from responding with sharp words encourages them to keep trying.

This kind of patience comes to us in small increments. It is the stuff of daily living, whether at work or in a family setting. We practice this virtue with varying degrees of success as we grow in disciplining our responses. We depend on mercy and forgiveness to continue growing in the virtuous life.

The *Catechism of the Catholic Church* offers us encouragement as we seek to grow in virtue:

> By this power of the Spirit, God's children can bear much fruit. He who has grafted us onto the true vine will make us bear "the fruit of the Spirit: . . . love, joy, peace, *patience,* kindness, goodness, faithfulness, gentleness, self-control." "We live by the Spirit"; the more we renounce ourselves, the more we "walk by the Spirit." (*CCC*, 736, quoting Galatians 5:22–23, 25; emphasis added)

Sometimes, however, we are called to a higher order of patience. The patient person bears suffering. We may face suffering in the form of physical or emotional challenges. This kind of suffering demands a mature patience coupled with perseverance to bear the suffering to its natural end. This kind of patience is built upon the foundation of hope, and strengthened by trust.

Patience depends upon trust. If we trust, truly trust the Lord, our waiting is a blessing, filled with the knowledge that God does in fact have us in the palm of his hand.

The Blessed Virgin Mary is the epitome of trust. From the very first moment of her *fiat,* she put her trust in the Lord and bore her suffering patiently, without complaint, without negotiating a different circumstance. Instead, she exhibited calm acceptance.

How difficult must is have been for her to face Joseph, pregnant and at his mercy?

How frightening was it to travel so close to giving birth and not know where she would rest?

How shocking must it have been to hear in the Temple that her own heart would one day be pierced?

And years later . . . how desperate and inconsolable must she have felt when holding the lifeless body of her son in her arms?

How does one bear these things patiently, if not with trust?

Jesus, I trust in you.

Consider the following as you think about the spiritual fruit of patience in your own life:

- Looking back on this past week, where can you see God exercising your "patience muscle"? What was the greatest challenge? Why?

- Is there one family member who seemed particularly well acquainted with your hot buttons? What is one thing you can do this week to show loving patience, even before it is needed?

- Maria spoke of trust as a necessary to cultivating patience. Why are those two things so closely connected, and how do you see these twin virtues revealing themselves in the story of the Visitation?

Reflect on the Meaning: The Visitation
by Alyssa Bormes

It was December 1, 1991, the first Sunday of Advent. My mother was at Mass with her eight children, and in his homily, the priest spoke about the unbearable waiting of Advent: that of an expectant mother in her last month of pregnancy—in this case, Mary anticipating Jesus—and the unknown day when Christ will come again. What Father didn't know was that my family was experiencing its own unbearable waiting.

Two days earlier my father, a doctor, had gone to visit his out-of-town nursing home patients. He lost control of his car on an icy curve; another car was unable to avoid him. The emergency crews extracted him from the car and rushed him the remaining twenty miles to the hospital.

Unsuspecting of anything being wrong, my mother had just welcomed her friend Sue for a cup of coffee when the phone call came. It began as a seemingly normal call: the hospital said that Dr. Bormes was in the emergency room. My mother thanked the caller, not understanding that this was not simply a courtesy call (someone would often call if my father was unexpectedly kept by an emergency). "No," the nurse persisted, her tone serious. "He is here in the emergency room. You need to come now."

We were in South Dakota, the neurosurgeon was in Minnesota, and another blizzard was hitting Minneapolis. My father's air-ambulance remained grounded while waiting for a break in the storm. After midnight, the plane left. An hour later a runway was plowed, allowing the plane to land, and the surgery took place in the middle of the night.

The next day, my mother and I arrived, followed by my siblings. On and on we waited. My father was on the ICU floor, where the patients in the most serious condition each had a nurse monitoring them twenty-four hours a day. The neurosurgeon told us that Dad was as stable as he could be now; as much as they knew about the brain, there was so much more that they didn't know. My father could awaken from his coma in days, weeks, months . . . or never again.

Gradually my siblings returned to their homes over the next days. Because I was already home in Minneapolis, my mother stayed with me. The days went by, each of them full of waiting. We could only be in my father's room for ten minutes of each hour, only two people could visit at a time, and the nurse was always present. Visitors came, calls came, and everyone waited as my father was experiencing his own manner of waiting in his coma. Would his brain heal itself?

Among the visitors was Bishop Paul Dudley. He and my father met when they were teenagers in the high school seminary. This visit went beyond friendship; His Excellency anointed my father as he remained in his silence.

A week had passed, and the prognosis hadn't changed: my father could awaken in days, weeks, months, or never, so we continued to wait. Then, later that evening, his brother—who was also Dr. Bormes—arrived and everything changed.

The nurse knew there was something special about this visit, so she waited just outside the sliding door. My uncle entered the room quietly with my aunt and my mother.

Then he began doing all sorts of things doctors do, like checking my father's reflexes. At last he spoke. "Bill, it's Bob. I'm here now."

Mom said my father began to shake and sweat; every alarm sounded on the machines. The nurse returned, telling them they had to leave so she could calm him. We all were to leave, even those of us in the waiting room, and not to return until the next day. At that time, some of us were certain that the unbearable waiting was soon to be over; he would awaken. However, the doctors among us that night, my uncle and brother, were quiet about the more likely outcome.

Late that night, we were told to return to the hospital. His death was imminent. We called my siblings who were not present and held the phone to my dad's ear for them to say goodbye. Then it was my turn. After telling him I loved him, I leaned to his ear and whispered, "Take care of my babies." He had known of one abortion, but, until that moment, I couldn't bring myself to tell him of the second.

The homily we had heard just days after my father's accident has never left my heart. There are so many times of waiting in life, at its beginning, all over in the middle, and at the end of life. No one is immune to the waiting. And no one is spared the suffering that goes with it, no matter how we try to shield ourselves.

Twenty-eight years ago, when I first learned I was pregnant, the prospect of waiting—especially the public waiting of the last few months, when I would be forced to endure the sidelong glances at my swollen belly and ringless finger—was more than I could bear. So I took my child's life.

Then, just over a year later, it happened again. And again I thought I couldn't bear the months of embarrassment and heartache, and so I made the worst possible choice. At the time, I was very far from the Church, and I had not yet found my way back the night of my father's death. Yet there was something so very piercing in that moment that I once again seized upon the truth he and my mother had taught me, the truth of Christ and his Church.

In those final moments with my father, I begged him to go on his own visitation, to be with my children, to care for them. God willing, he is holding them now along with three of his own children, the three who died before birth.

This Advent, the waiting is no longer one of dread but of hope. My heart still aches with longing for my father, for my children, and now for my mother who has died. However, in my heart I entrust them all to Mary, our Mother, who gave the gift of her son. And in him there is hope for the final visitation, the day, God willing, we will all be reunited in heaven. This magnificent hope, at times seemingly endless, flowers inside us, so that the waiting is no longer unbearable.

While every child is a gift from God, the news of an unexpected pregnancy can strike fear in the hearts of those who are already struggling, perhaps especially those who are already raising other children alone. The story of the Visitation is a story of two women—one not yet married, the other infertile—who entrusted this most intimate part of themselves to God, confident that he would make a way. And yet, too many women hold on to their fear and resentment, unable to trust in the goodness of the gift.

As you are reading this, someone is weighed down, facing the choice of a lifetime. Take a moment to pray for her, right now. Maybe it's someone you know. Maybe it's you. Know that at this moment, your sisters are holding this dear sister before the throne of grace. Life is precious. Handle with prayer. —Kelly Wahlquist

Visio Divina: Contemplate the Lord through Sacred Images

by Dr. Elizabeth Lev and Kelly Wahlquist

Bernardino Pinturicchio, *Visitation*, ca. 1494–1496. Photo ©
Vatican Museums. All rights reserved.

The image for this *visio divina* exercise is *Visitation* by Bernardino Pinturicchio (1494). The original hangs in the Borgia Apartments of the Vatican Museums in Rome.

    Fifteenth-century Italian Renaissance painter Bernardino di Betto, nicknamed "Pinturicchio" (meaning "little painter") on account of his diminutive size, worked for no fewer than four popes. Hugely popular for his ability to entwine brilliant colors with three-dimensional elements such as metal, wax, and gold leaf, he produced works so intricately ornate they made it seem as if one was stepping into an illuminated manuscript. His dazzling *Visitation* was executed in the suite of six rooms in the Vatican known as the Borgia Apartments.

Find the color image of Pinturicchio's *Visitation* at the front of the book. Spend a few moments gazing on it before returning to the reflection. Use a bookmark to hold your place so you can return to it easily.

Focus your attention on the characters in the painting, noticing their expressions and movements and the colors, spaces, and shapes that surround them. Ask the Holy Spirit to help you look with the eyes of a prayerful wonderer, and contemplate what you see.

The image sparkles with light and detail like the joyful mystery it is—a bit like music or even the Magnificat itself. The scene is a very feminine one, as evidenced by the many women immersed in various nurturing activities. The center of the fresco draws our attention to the person who is the first to recognize the presence of her Redeemer in the womb of her young cousin and in cheerful humility joyfully proclaim the Incarnation: "And why is this granted me, that the mother of my Lord should come to me?" (Lk 1:43).

Pinturicchio has placed Elizabeth front and center for a reason, for at this moment she holds an important role in salvation history; she is a beautiful witness of how we can recognize, respond to, and rejoice in the proclamation of the Gospel. Mary, draped in the blue mantle of the Queen of Heaven, enters into her cousin's tender embrace as Joseph waits lovingly off to the side. As you take in the ornate colors, notice the setting, the characters surrounding Mary and Elizabeth, and their actions.

Place yourself in the scene. Imagine you are one of the onlookers watching and hearing the joyful proclamation of coming of the Christ from the lips of a woman you have always known as kind, righteous, and patient. What verbal and nonverbal signs between these two cousins do you observe?

Stay in that moment; meditate on the Visitation, and reflect upon your own life. What interaction do you see between these two women that resembles a relationship you have with a spiritual mother, spiritual daughter, or sister in Christ? Ask the Lord to bless that unique relationship and to show you how such a relationship is capable of bearing Christ to the world.

Questions for Group Discussion
by Dr. Carol Younger

Below are questions relating to various sections of the chapter to help each member of the small group grow in knowledge and faith. —Kelly Wahlquist

1. Walk with Mary toward Elizabeth for just a moment. She longed for the Messiah to come. Elizabeth longed for it also. Now the Messiah *is* coming, and Elizabeth's deep desire is coming to fruition—she is with child. With God, all things are possible! What will Mary tell you about the deep desires of your heart? What do you think is impossible yet you patiently ask him for over and over? Might you make it a little more real by sharing it?

2. When was the last time you shouted aloud with joy? Joy! When was the last time you experienced such an insight into God's great love for you that your soul erupted with a cry of joy, sometimes including tears? What was

that moment? Pray through its details, nuances of meaning, and all the tiny aspects of that event. Now, retell that joy to someone new, to your group. In the retelling, share your gratitude to God for the experience. *That* is the *Magnificat* moment. That is Mary's song.

3. Even Elizabeth may have had her doubts about the good to come in the future. Elizabeth would surely look you straight in the eye and admit she doubted the savior would come to her backwater town. What location, situation, or problem (personal or public) have you looked at saying: "Surely the Lord will not be concerned at all about this." The hidden savior in Mary's womb did concern himself with Elizabeth! What surprising intervention of the Lord have you seen when you prayed as Elizabeth did: "My trust is in the Lord. I will wait on his faithfulness"? What have you waited and waited for and found it in the Lord's faithfulness?

4. Tired though she may be, Elizabeth responds immediately to the need for charity for the poor at her door. And she is rewarded! The Holy Spirit pours out from her toward Mary, who is looking at her: "Blessed are you who believed that what was spoken you by the Lord would be fulfilled." Think about someone you pray with and pray for, someone who has just brought her good news to you. Of course, you congratulate her, and together you praise the Lord in joy! What did she say? What did you reply? What prayer in faith of yours has been answered? Share the joy with your friends and the group!

Walking in the New Evangelization
by Kelly Wahlquist

As we conclude this chapter, think about how each aspect has spoken to your heart. What have the scriptures revealed to you? Which qualities of the women in the story resonated with you? How have your eyes been opened to walking in patience? Here are a couple of ways you can continue to reflect upon what you have discovered and grow in virtue.

Virtue in Action

Sometimes patience gets mixed up with discouragement. We tell ourselves it's just not possible for God to answer our requests or that we don't have enough faith for God to grant them. "It just wasn't meant to be," we say.

Did Elizabeth feel that way, after waiting so many years for God to answer her prayer for a child? Elizabeth had been patient and faithful, and you can be too. One way to grow in the virtue of patience is to make an act of trust: tell Jesus that you will accept dependence on him, on his will for your life, in *his time*. Believe, entrust yourself to Jesus, and simply pray: "My Jesus, I trust you. I believe you have only good planned for me; help me to humbly and patiently accept your will in each moment, each day of my life until I see you in eternal joy." And when you are given to impatience, simply pray, "Jesus, I trust in you."

Until next time, may the joyful patience of Elizabeth take root and grow in your heart.

3.

Gaze with Charity

(The Nativity)

A Moment to Ponder

by Kelly Wahlquist

In his great eucharistic prayer, *Adoro te devote*, St. Thomas Aquinas wrote about approaching the Lord in the monstrance just as the shepherds and the Magi presented themselves to the infant King: humbly, on bended knee. His lyric, translated by Gerard Manley Hopkins, S.J., overflows with love, focused with laser-sharp precision on the miracle before him.

> Adoro te devote, latens Deitas,
> Quæ sub his figuris vere latitas;
> Tibi se cor meum totum subjicit,
> Quia te contemplans totum deficit.

> Godhead here in hiding, whom I do adore,
> Masked by these bare shadows, shape and nothing more.
> See, Lord, at Thy service low lies here a heart
> Lost, all lost in wonder in the God thou art.[1]

As we approach—whether in the manger in our hearts or in the monstrance on our knees—we cannot help but get caught up in the wonder of it all ourselves: that "God so loved the world that he gave his only Son" (Jn 3:16). And in that sending, we find at once the greatest proof of love himself and the most persuasive reason to give ourselves wholeheartedly to worship the One who presents himself there, lowly and helpless—all for love of us.

Enter the Scripture
by Sarah Christmyer

Read Luke 2:1–20 before you start.

From where I stood on the stairs, I could hear my grandmother's friends gathering in the living room for her eightieth birthday. As I rounded the landing and came into sight, they suddenly stopped. Six pairs of eyes fixed on my fifteen-year-old face. Finally, one woman broke the silence. "Why, Grace [my grandma's name]: *here thee is!*" The genteel Quaker "thee" underlined their impression. In me, they saw their childhood friend.

"The apple doesn't fall far from the tree," as the saying goes, and they say I am like my grandma Grace in demeanor as well as in looks. Similarly, my husband, Mark, and I see flashes of our parents in our four children. If this is true for us humans, how much more so must the Son of God reflect the Father?

"No one has ever seen God; the only Son . . . has made him known" (Jn 1:18).

At the birth of Jesus, the previously invisible God became visible, vulnerably so. We can only imagine what Mary thought as she gazed on her newborn son. I remember searching my own babies' faces for hints of their father and me. Did Mary look past what she saw of her own features, trying to catch a glimpse of the divine?

Luke says more about the circumstances around Jesus' birth than he says about what the Child looked like. Here are some things that stand out.

God Really Did Become a Man, Born of a Woman

He entered our world at a particular time and place. Luke tells us that Joseph and Mary were registered in the worldwide census ordered by Caesar Augustus when Quirinius was governor of Syria (ca. 51 BC—AD 21).[2] The reality of his existence was attested to in the annals of the first-century Jewish historian Josephus.

Jesus Is the True Prince of Peace!

At the time Joseph and Mary were answering the decree of Caesar Augustus, heading to Bethlehem to be enrolled, Caesar was proclaimed throughout the Roman Empire as the "son of god." Caesar worship was the official religion. Augustus was celebrated as savior of the world and for ushering in peace and prosperity (what we call the *Pax Romana*). A calendar inscription from 9 BC proclaims Caesar's birth to be the beginning of the new year and that it is the *euangelion*, "good news," for the entire empire.[3] So when Jesus was born, the Roman world was worshiping a son of god who brings good news and peace to all . . . whose name was Caesar Augustus.

In light of this, just think what the angelic message must have sounded like to those simple Jewish shepherds: "I bring you *good news* . . . for to you is born this day . . . *a Savior*. . . . 'Glory to God in the highest, and *on earth peace among men!*'" (Lk 2:10, 11, 14; emphasis added).

Caesar Augustus may have brought good news and peace, to a certain extent. But the peace God brings through his Son is a peace Caesar couldn't begin to imagine or bring.[4] And the Good News of God's salvation is eternal.

We Are Meant to Notice the Manger

Luke mentions it three times in three paragraphs, like a chorus. Yes, the manger gives the shepherds a way to recognize the baby. And yes, the manger points to Jesus' humble beginnings. But a "manger" in "Bethlehem"—there's a heavenly significance in the fact that God's son is born in the "House of Bread" (which is what "Bethlehem" means) and laid in a feeding trough. Already at his birth there are hints that Jesus will become bread to feed the world.

Notice the Swaddling Cloths

They may not sound royal to us, but the way Luke describes Jesus' wrapping recalls the biblical words of a son of David, Solomon, about his own humble birth: "I was nursed with care in swaddling cloths. For no king has had a different beginning of existence" (Ws 7:4–5).

Together, the manger and the swaddling cloths point to Jesus' end and the reason that he came to earth. The strips of linen used to swaddle babies were also used to wrap bodies before burial. So there's a nice symmetry to the fact that Jesus is "wrapped in swaddling cloths" and "laid" in a stone manger in Luke 2, and then "wrapped in a linen shroud" and "laid" in a rock-hewn tomb in Luke 23:53. Jesus takes our "clothes" to the grave, and we who are reborn in him rise clothed in his life at the resurrection.

What kind of king chooses to be born among shepherds and laid in a manger? One who "did not count equality with God a thing to be grasped"—what a contrast with the kings of our world!—"but emptied himself, taking the form of a servant, being born in the likeness of men . . . and [becoming] obedient unto death, even death on a cross" (Phil 2:6–8).

The death of Jesus is far in the future, but its shadow falls on the manger. None who see him in those early days know that, however. They know he is the promised king. They praise and give glory to God. They wonder. And Mary "kept all these things, pondering them in her heart" (Lk 2:19).

We can picture the shepherds gathered around the manger. The baby sleeps, so they turn to the mother, whose eyes are fixed on his face. "Who does he look like?" they might ask. "Behold," I imagine her to think, though not to say: "his is the face of God." The One who gave Mary his image has taken her flesh.

Prayer

Lord, I want to see Jesus! Jesus—show me the Father! With your gaze, draw me into your eternal exchange of love.

Gaze Upon Jesus: Lila, the Innkeeper's Servant

A story by Stephanie Landsem

Don't be afraid. I rubbed the softest spot between the little ewe's twitching ears.

I knew about being afraid. But, like my master said, I didn't know much about anything else—especially about birthing a lamb. I wished hard for Isaac. If he were here, he'd know what to do. My brother is younger than I, but he is smart. I am older—past the age when girls get married—and simple. No one would marry someone simple and ugly and lame like me. The master said that, too.

"Lila!" The master's voice sounded from the house. The way he said it meant if I didn't hurry, I'd get a beating.

Sahbah bumped his nose into my back, snuffling his concern, but the donkey couldn't help this ewe any more than I could. Doves flapped in the beams above my head; their soft coos showed that they were anxious, too. The stable was a dry place, safe from the wind. It was the place I liked the most when I wasn't with Isaac. I slept here, with the donkey I called Sahbah—he had a whiskery, gray nose like a grandfather—and the ox I just called Ox. The doves liked to flutter down and perch on my hands and shoulders if I stayed very, very still. The animals loved me, but not like Isaac loved me. I know animals can't love like people can.

"You c-can do it," I urged the ewe as she rolled her eyes and shuddered.

I might be simple and ugly and lame, but I wouldn't leave the little ewe by herself to have her baby. The ewe made a soft bleat. A scared sound. I petted her more fiercely. She twitched, and her bloated stomach heaved as a shiny bundle slipped from her onto the straw.

"Good g-g-girl." I kissed her between her wet black eyes. I hadn't done anything but sit beside her, but I felt a warmth in my chest like I did when Isaac told me I'd done something right.

The little bundle lay still. My heart sank down hard. I took a handful of straw and rubbed the lamb like I'd seen Isaac do. It didn't move. I pulled open its tiny mouth, leaned down and waited to feel soft breath on my cheek. Nothing.

"Li-LA!" Master's voice was angry now.

The ewe nosed the lamb and then turned away.

Tears pricked the backs of my eyes. What had I done wrong? I sat beside the tiny lamb, waiting. I'd waited like this before, beside Mama. Waited so long for her to wake up. I had held Mama's hand, calling to her. Then Isaac had told me about *dead*. It meant Mama would never open her eyes again. Would never hold me tight or sing to me. My chest got tight and I couldn't breathe. I felt like that a lot. Tight and heavy and sad. Afraid. And alone, since Isaac went away. And now the little lamb was dead, just like Mama. The ewe lay down in the straw. Did she feel alone and sad? Did dead mean the same to sheep as it did to me?

After a long time of waiting, I wrapped the cold, still body in a scrap of cloth just like they had wrapped Mama in tight, white cloths after she stopped moving and breathing. *I'm sorry.* I petted the ewe again. *I'm sorry I didn't know what to do.*

Isaac hadn't wanted to leave me here after Mama died. He told the master I'd work hard in the house and stable while he took care of the flocks outside the walls. Isaac told me the master would feed me and give me a place to sleep if I was good and worked hard. I tried. I tried to pour the wine without spilling and to empty the night jars before the master woke in the morning. But sometimes my withered hand didn't work. Sometimes my lame leg hurt and made me slow. Sometimes I didn't remember. And then the master got angry.

I tried not to cry when Isaac visited me, but I couldn't help it. "Why can't I go with you?"

"I've told you, Lila," he said in his soft voice. He always talked softly to me. Not like the master or the travelers who came and went from the house. "It's dangerous outside the walls of the city." He told me about people who jumped out of the night with clubs and knives. Of men who would kill for food. Of wild animals who attacked the sheep. What he said made me afraid. I didn't want him to be dead, like Mama. I held on to him tight before he left. But I remembered what he said and never went outside the walls to find him, no matter how lonely I was.

I buried the lamb far away from the cave. Prayer was not looked on kindly in my master's home, but I whispered a plea to the God Mama had prayed to. The one in the Temple. *God, why did the lamb have to die? Why did Mama have to die and leave us?* But Mama's God didn't answer me.

I ran back to check on the ewe, giving her water and food and a clean bed before I went to my master to get the beating that was coming to me. It hurt, but not as bad as the tight hurt in my chest when I thought of the still little lamb.

When the sun went down, I served my master and those who had come to stay in his house bread and meat and watered wine. Plenty of water and not much wine, just like the master told me. The men talked about the census, like they usually did. My master called it a godsend. I thought Caesar had ordered the census, not a god. But when I said that, my master laughed in the way I didn't like and told me I wasn't good at thinking and shouldn't do it. "But w-w-why does Caesar need to count us?" I asked. I could count, but not past twelve, and there were many more than twelve in Bethlehem.

"To keep the *Pax Romana*," he said, not even looking up from his stew of goat meat.

"The Romans b-b-bring peace?" I wasn't sure what peace was, but it didn't seem like there was any in Bethlehem. Crowded streets and angry merchants, soldiers who pushed and shouted orders. And here, at my master's house, weary travelers gave him silver coins to sleep on the roof and the floor and even in the courtyard.

"Augustus brings peace, you stupid woman," my master said. "That's what the decree says. And we must pay for the peace with tribute. And for tribute, we must be counted."

I nodded, but I didn't understand much except that the Roman's peace had filled my master's purse with silver.

I stacked the dirty cups on the serving tray and lurched toward the courtyard, balancing the tray against my uneven walk, careful not to drop it. I remembered a feeling I had, when Mama wasn't dead, when she held me tight and sang to me. It might have been peace. I almost felt it again sometimes, when I curled up beside Sahbah and Ox at night, my work done, their breath warming the cave. Sometimes, the coo of the doves sounded almost like Mama singing me to sleep. But in the morning when I woke up, the feeling was gone and the cold tight feeling was back. Mama was dead, and Isaac was far away in the fields. That was the sad, alone feeling.

It was dark by the time I finished my work. The travelers began to spread their cloaks and blankets on the floor and roof of the house. Soon, they would all sleep and I could go to the quiet of the stable. I was hungry, and so were the doves and Sahbah and Ox. I had a few crusts for the doves and a bit of meat and bread for myself. Sahbah and Ox and the ewe would get the master's grain, and we would curl up and keep each other warm.

A knock sounded on the courtyard gate.

My master said a word I'd heard many times but knew I shouldn't say myself. He downed the last of his wine and waved a hand at me. "Answer it, woman. And tell them there isn't a corner to be had in this house."

I limped to the door. Whoever it was shouldn't be in the streets after dark; even I knew that. I pulled open the heavy door. A man stood before me, a small oil lamp in his hand throwing flickering shadows on his dusty clothes and worried face.

I shook my head. "I'm s-s-sorry. We have no room."

His shoulders drooped. "We've been all over the city." He seemed like a kind man. He didn't look at my withered arm and make a face like other people did. He looked behind him. A woman sat on a donkey. She was pretty. And then I saw—as she rubbed her back as if it hurt her—her stomach was rounded out like a water jar. She had a baby in her. Her face was pale in the moonlight, and she looked weary and a little afraid. Like my little ewe.

"M-m-master? The woman is w-w-with child." Surely he would find them a place.

He roared his most angry roar, making me jump. "Send them away and put down the beam, woman."

My face got hot. Master was wrong to turn them away, but I couldn't go against him. I closed the gate and put the beam in place, my heart hurting for the man and the woman with the baby. I wished hard—so hard—to know what to do. Then, suddenly, I had an idea.

Master wouldn't like it. But I thought maybe he wouldn't know if I was careful. I limped through the house and slipped out the back door like I was going to the stable for sleep. But I didn't. I went out into the street. I hoped they hadn't gone too far. They couldn't go out the city gate, not in the night with the bad men and wild animals. I tried to run but it was more like a lopsided hop. Then I saw them.

I reached the man and grabbed at his cloak. "W-w-wait."

He turned to me, surprise in his lined face.

"I . . . d-d-don't . . ." Now that I stood before the man and his wife, my idea seemed foolish. They might even be angry. Maybe they didn't like animals.

"Please," the man said, "her time is near." His voice was soft like Isaac's.

I dared to glance at the woman. Her hands cradled her swelled belly, her eyes were weary, but she smiled. At me. It was a pretty smile, like Mama's. I turned back toward my master's house. "F-f-follow me."

I brought them a jar of clean water and spread my blanket on a pile of fresh straw. Mary—she told me that was her name and the man was Joseph—gripped my hand hard. She was breathing fast and her face was shiny with sweat. "I can fetch a woman, s-s-someone to help." But I didn't know who, or where.

"Stay with me, Lila," Mary said. I think she knew it would be soon.

My heart pounded hard. Would it be like my ewe? Would the baby come out quiet and still?

But it wasn't like that. Not one bit. I think my heart stopped when the baby came out. But the little one moved and breathed. Its hands were clenched in little fists, and it let out a cry that started my heart beating again.

"A son," I said, and for once my tongue did not stumble. I set him, naked and mewing, into his mother's arms. I felt that feeling again, like my chest was swelling up with warm air.

Mary motioned to the pack they'd brought with them. "Clothes, to wrap him," she said.

It was a little bit like when I'd wrapped the little lamb or when they'd wrapped Mama. Except this little baby was alive and breathing and making noises. I spread the clothes on the soft straw. Mary laid the squirming baby on top. He pulled his legs up into his chest. I gently pushed his legs down, but he pulled them back up. Mary showed me how to wrap each side of the cloth snug and tucked it around him. He quieted. I scooped him up and settled him in Mary's arms.

Then . . . I don't think anyone would believe what happened then. I don't even believe it, and I'm simple and a fool.

The baby, he opened his eyes and looked at me.

It was like the sun had come up, right in the cave, like a flood of warm, bright light. All the shadows disappeared. The stink of animals and dirt went away, and the air filled with the smell of roses. Sahbah stopped his snuffling, and the doves stopped their cooing and fluttering. Everything stopped.

Where my heart beat in my chest, I felt something loosen and come free. The sad tight feeling I'd carried since Mama . . . it slipped away and the warm light filled the place where it had been. I felt Mama's arms around me, her voice in my ear, telling me she loved me.

I wanted everything to stay stopped. I wanted Mama to stay with me. But the bright flood of light faded. The doves cooed, and Sahbah shifted in the straw. Mary set the baby in Sahbah's manger, and Joseph came to stand beside her.

Yet the feeling in my chest didn't go away. The tight sadness didn't come back. The bright warmth settled inside me. This was what peace was. Not the kind that came from soldiers or a man called Caesar.

This was inside peace.

I think Mary and Joseph felt it, too, because they didn't talk. They just looked at the child with their faces all lit up like they had a light inside them. Like the light I felt glowing inside me.

I don't know how long I stood there, feeling the inside peace. Feeling Mama's love. Then, I thought of Isaac. He needed to feel the inside peace. He needed to hear Mama's voice, too.

I jumped up. "I'll c-c-come back soon." I wasn't supposed to go out of the city walls. I'd promised. But this was different. This was Mama and the warm light and making the sadness go away.

I cut through the streets of Bethlehem as fast as I could, not even minding the ache in my leg. The streets smelled like donkeys and smoke. Oil lamps flickered from windows and lit the way. At the city gate, the watchman was asleep. I pushed open the side door, and I was outside. I stopped, my heart pounding hard. It was dark. So dark. The wind cut through my thin mantle. How could I find Isaac in the dark? And what about the wild animals and men with clubs and knives?

Then a light cut through the dark. I looked up, but it wasn't the moon. It was a star. A silver star bright enough to light the path. A warm light. A light that made me not afraid. I scrambled along the path, stumbling on roots and rocks. I crested a rocky hillside, and the star lit a flock of sheep clustered and quiet in the lee of the valley. Men huddled beside a fire. Isaac was there.

He saw me and jumped up. "Lila?"

He ran toward me, and I tried to think of what to say. About the baby and Mama and the smell of roses. What if he didn't believe me? What if he wouldn't leave his flock? But before I said a word, the sheep began to cry out like frightened children. The other shepherds leapt to their feet, reaching for their staffs. Isaac turned to the hills, his eyes searching the darkness for the danger.

But it wasn't danger. It was the star. The one that had lit my way. It was growing brighter and brighter, like the sun rising in the middle of the night. The men raised their arms to protect themselves. But I knew that light. It was the same warm light that had filled the cave. The light that filled me and Joseph and Mary. A sound like wind and water rushed all around us. Isaac pulled me close, as if to save me, but I wasn't afraid. The roar turned into the sound of bells, silvery and bright.

"Be not afraid," the bells said.

Isaac was looking up at the light. I looked up, too. It didn't hurt my eyes, not like looking at the sun. And just like when I looked at the baby's face, I never wanted to look away.

The voice of the bells came again. "Behold, I bring you good news of a great joy which will come to all the people; for to you is born this day in the city of David a Savior, who is Christ the Lord."

The bells were talking about the baby. Mary and Joseph's baby. I wanted to tell Isaac I knew the baby, the one they meant. But he was frozen like a statue, looking at the star.

"And this will be a sign for you: you will find a babe wrapped in swaddling cloths and lying in a manger." Suddenly, the star was joined by more stars until the sky was on fire—silver bells singing and trumpets calling, "Glory to God in the highest, and on earth peace among men with whom he is pleased!"

I didn't know how long the bells and trumpets went on, but then the bright star faded, the cold and dark came back, and the sheep shifted restlessly. Isaac had fallen down, but he got back up. The other shepherds looked like they'd just woken up from a dream. "We must go," Isaac said, "to find this child."

"But where?" a shepherd pushed himself up on his staff. "How can we find an infant in the whole city? Where do we look?"

Isaac shook his head, and for the first time in my life, I knew what others didn't. I knew what to do. I knew where the baby was. I had wrapped him in the clothes. I had looked on his face. My words came out just right. "I know."

Isaac would hear Mama's voice and have the warm light in his heart. The inside peace that came from gazing at the baby.

"I know where the baby is. Follow me."

In Search of Charity: The Nativity
by Maria Morera Johnson

"Charity is the theological virtue by which we love God above all things for his own sake, and our neighbor as ourselves for the love of God" (CCC, 1822). It is the single most important characteristic by which the Christian is known, for love is the ultimate source of all goodness, truth, and beauty—and to the degree that we grow in love, we gain a clearer view of what heaven will be. In the Nativity, love reached down from heaven and made its mark on the human race. And on no one was that mark more visible than the first to bear witness to his presence in the world: his own mother. —Kelly Wahlquist

My office is filled with images of Our Lady of Charity of El Cobre, the patroness of my birthplace, Cuba. A small statue, a modern painting, and numerous cards and kitschy items remind me, everywhere I look, that Mary is watching over me.

The work of a writer is lonesome, and sometimes lonely, so to catch a glimpse of the Blessed Virgin Mary reminds me that I am not alone, and that I belong to her, and to her son, Jesus Christ.

Just as I love to visit with family and friends, so does Mary! From that first moment when she visited Elizabeth, carrying Jesus in her womb, she began to bring her love—and the Incarnation of Love: her son, Jesus Christ—to others.

When I catch a glimpse of one of the little icons in my office, it serves me just as well—a reminder of Love. And just as she visits with me, Mary visits with all those who care to look for her, in grand and public ways such as the approved apparitions of Fatima and Guadalupe (and others!), and in private ways, perhaps as we pray or sit peacefully.

I grew up knowing Mary under this title of Our Lady of Charity, but in my family, when speaking of the Blessed Mother, we called her "la virgencita," *the little virgin.* The diminutive had nothing to do with her size but rather was a sweet and affectionate term, not unlike calling her "Mommy." It was later, as an adult, that I connected charity with love. Of course! This title of Mary is Our Lady of Love! How fitting.

The *Catechism of the Catholic Church* tells us that "Charity is the soul of the holiness to which all are called: 'it governs, shapes, and perfects all the means of sanctification'" (CCC, 826). Without love, we couldn't possibly grow in any of the other virtues we aspire to perfect. Quoting St. Thérèse of Lisieux, the *Catechism* continues:

If the Church was a body composed of different members, it couldn't lack the noblest of all; *it must have a
Heart, and a Heart BURNING WITH LOVE.* And I realized that *this love alone* was the true motive force which
enabled the other members of the Church to act; if it
ceased to function, the Apostles would forget to preach
the gospel, the Martyrs would refuse to shed their
blood. LOVE, IN FACT, IS THE VOCATION WHICH
INCLUDES ALL OTHERS; IT'S A UNIVERSE OF ITS
OWN, COMPRISING ALL TIME AND SPACE—IT'S
ETERNAL![5]

I am inspired by the selfless love evident in the Nativity. Some of the early Church fathers taught that, because
she was sinless, Mary did not experience the pain of childbirth that most women do. Even if this is true, Mary and
Joseph both sacrificed greatly, out of love for God, to be
instruments in the hands of the Lord and to parent the Son
of God. They surrendered their own human desires for
intimacy, their reputations, and even their personal safety
to love, protect, and share their lives with Love Incarnate.

Though the details of their intimate communion are
only hinted at in the pages of scripture, we know that the
Holy Family experienced tremendous graces because of
their faithfulness and that they pray for us, asking God to
grant us a measure of the charity that graced their lives, that
we, too, might bring Jesus to the world around us.

Consider the following as you think about the virtue of
charity and how you have been cultivating it in your own
life:

• Think about the concrete, tangible ways you show your
love for those around you—family, friends, and others
who are important to you. What are some of the ways

you show your love for God? How are they different? How are they similar?

- The *Catechism* says that we are to show charity (love) for others, out of love for God. How does this motivating force make a difference?

- In this reflection, Maria talks of the many ways the Blessed Mother reveals herself to her children. What is your favorite form, and why?

Reflect on the Meaning: The Nativity
by Katie Warner

When I was a young girl, I remember the pastor at my childhood church often reminding us, "At every moment, do what love requires." It wasn't until I had waded the waters of family life that I came to have a true understanding of what that adage meant.

I was a fairly abnormal sixteen year old. Having been deeply energized in my faith at age thirteen, during eucharistic adoration, I spent the following teenage years wearing a giant crucifix around my neck, carrying around devotionals or books from the saints, and waiting for the next chance to talk to someone about Jesus. I craved volunteer opportunities, Bible studies, and evangelism.

Honestly, loving others was fairly easy for me. Sometimes it required a little awkwardness or vulnerability, and quite often it meant a big dose of making a fool of myself if the person to whom I was speaking was radically disinterested in the Christian walk, but for the most part, I didn't have to sacrifice a lot to love those around me.

When I began my work in ministry—speaking and writing nationally, in addition to working part-time for the media apostolate Catholics Come Home—I also found it invigorating to practice charity toward others as part of my evangelization work. Love was almost always a joy and never took too much work. I *thought* I knew what charity looked like in practice. This was it! Look at the fruits of this evangelization work! Look how many people I can share the truth and joy of Jesus with! Look at the time I can spend in God's Word, in eucharistic adoration, getting involved in parish ministry . . .

I married in my early twenties, and as I write this, I'm pregnant with our third child. Family life is where the story changed for me, where love had to be put into serious practice. Family life showed me that love isn't always easy, that it practically demands growth, and that possessing great charity isn't a life goal but rather a *moment-by-moment* work. Our pastor didn't say "Over the course of your life, do what love requires"—but rather "at *every moment*."

Close your eyes for a moment, and imagine the scene of the Nativity. It's peaceful—albeit a little farm-smelly—but oh so full of love. It reminds me of my own first encounter with my son after his birth, husband at my side, filled with more love for my family than I could have ever imagined feeling on this side of eternity.

And yet, this moment at the manger—this idyllic scene with the Christ Child and his parents—was just one moment in the life of the Holy Family. They lived the virtue of charity dynamically, at *every* moment.

Some of my moments at home? Not so charitable. St. Teresa of Calcutta once said, "It is easy to love the people far away. It is not always easy to love those close to us. It is easier to give a cup of rice to relieve hunger than to relieve the loneliness and pain of someone unloved in our own home. Bring love into your home, for this is where our love for each other must start."[6]

Isn't that true? I remember being really angry with my husband one night over something that, in hindsight, was fueled by my own frustrations in the moment. I did *not* want to do what love required in that moment—to lay down my pride, to forgive, to show mercy, and to exhibit sanctifying charity. Instead I grabbed a favorite spiritual book in one hand, a rosary in the other, and I prayed for the Holy Family to soften my heart and replace bitterness with charity. I've realized many times that this is a prayer that the Holy Family loves to hear and answer, as my vitriol quickly melted into a meekness of heart that could not have come of my own feeble human strength.

The good news is, we don't have to look far to see how to "do what love requires" in every moment we are given, especially when we interact with the people closest to us. We know how love acts, *what love requires*, because scripture tells us in 1 Corinthians: "Love is patient and kind; love is not jealous or boastful; it is not arrogant or rude. Love does not insist on its own way; it is not irritable or resentful; it does not rejoice at wrong, but rejoices in the right. Love bears all things, believes all things, hopes all things, endures all things" (1 Cor 13:4–7).

Love is patient when the toddler is screaming on the floor in the supermarket.

Love is kind when your spouse forgets (again) to do something you've asked.

Love is not jealous when your sibling or friend catches a break you long to have.

Love is not rude when you can't have your way.

Love—at *every moment*—bears all the things that weigh you down, believes all things related to God's incredible plan for you and your family (that you often can't see yourself), hopes all things about God's desire to bring you prosperity through the often-unseen, nitty-gritty work of love in family life. Love *at every moment* endures all things, all bumps and bruises and tears and shouts of joy and laughter along the way.

Charity is the mother of all virtues and the virtue *this* mother certainly needs most, because loving those closest to me in all of those tiny moments spread out before me—emulating in some small way the perfect charity of the Holy Family—is what's going to get me—and you—to heaven.

- Go back and read that passage from 1 Corinthians 13 again, slowly. Substitute your name for the word "love." Is there any part of this reading that doesn't ring true? What do you need to do to cultivate that expression of love?

- God creates each of us with different personalities and gifts. What was easy for Katie—sharing her faith openly and enthusiastically with strangers—might not come naturally to you. Can you think of a time this week—or next week—when you have had (or will have) an opportunity to "do what love requires in the moment"?

Visio Divina: Contemplate the Lord through Sacred Images

by Dr. Elizabeth Lev and Kelly Wahlquist

Giovanni di Paolo, *The Nativity*, 1440. Photo © Vatican Museums. All rights reserved.

The image for this *visio divina* exercise is called *The Nativity*, by Giovanni di Paolo (1440). The original hangs in the Vatican Museums' Pinacoteca (Painting Gallery) in Rome.

One of the last artists to embrace the tradition of medieval painting, Giovanni di Paolo used colorful and at times exaggerated figures and landscapes to veer the onlooker from objective reality and arouse a subjective emotional response. His graceful elongated figures, inspired by the mystical images of contemporary Fra Angelico, rejected the popular action-driven scenes in favor of inviting wonder and contemplation.

Find the color image of Giovanni di Paolo's *The Nativity* at the front of the book. Spend a few moments gazing on it before returning to the reflection. Use a bookmark to hold your place so you can return to it easily.

Focus your attention on the characters in the painting, noticing their expressions and movements, and the colors, spaces, and shapes that surround them. Ask the Holy Spirit to help you look with the eyes of a prayerful wonderer and contemplate what you see.

The Light of the World penetrates darkness, and so in this nocturnal scene depicting the Nativity, light exudes not from ordinary sources but rather from heaven itself. The central characters are illuminated by the warm glow of the rays emanating from the Infant Jesus, who is the Light that shines in the darkness (see John 1:5), while beams of light shine down from heaven upon the shepherds as the angel announces the birth of the Savior.

The earthly elements in the setting are depicted realistically, yet each is rich with symbolism—and the contrast draws us to contemplate the mystery of the Incarnation: of the God who so loved us that he became one of us in order to redeem us and who did it in a humble and unexpected way, as a newborn babe.

Turn your focus to that which surrounds the Holy Family, and contemplate the otherworldly qualities each holds. Notice the ox and the donkey. Look beyond their earthly characteristics and see them in light of the prophecies of

Isaiah that speak of a Savior (see Isaiah 1:3). A simple flower depicts two of God's greatest acts of mercy. The color of the red roses can symbolize Christ's Passion and Death, while the fact that they are flowering in December symbolizes Christ's birth.

Now turn your attention to the women in the painting. What is their role? What virtues do they portray? Put yourself in the scene as one of the women. How have you helped bring Jesus into the world? What have you just experienced? Imagine the transformation that would take place in your heart as you witnessed the incarnation of Love! With a heart on fire for the love of Jesus, where will you go from here? Who will you tell?

Questions for Group Discussion
by Dr. Carol Younger

Below are questions from various sections of the chapter to help each member of the small group grow in knowledge and faith.
—Kelly Wahlquist

1. Who do you look like in your birth family? If your fifteen-year-old self were to walk into a room, what person would hear, *"Why* [your relative], *here thee is!"* Now, think deeper; whom do you most resemble, in virtue, in your family? Name that person's virtue and loving actions (such as charity toward others). What are *your* strengths? And yes, what is *your* charity? Thank God here in this group, aloud, bravely, naming your areas where others get a glimpse of his love through your actions.

2. Do you see Jesus' manger and swaddling clothes? Someone looked after you as an infant just as Mary looked after Jesus. That person (likely your mother) smiled and

cooed at you while feeding you and changing you. She delighted in seeing you grow and become an independent nourisher of others and a charitable changer of lives. What memory from your childhood has additional meaning (and even prophetic nuances) for your life now? How do you now notice and respond to others' needs, at the beginning of life or at the end?

3. *"The baby, he opened his eyes and he looked at me."* The excitement of a newborn seen through eyes of a simple girl who doesn't know the story of salvation! Think back to the first Christmas you remember: What do you see? Who told you the story of Christ's birth the first time? How did you tell your (or others') children about baby Jesus? How did you make it exciting? How did their faces look? Share some memory of your excitement at a family Christmas celebration.

4. Lila looks at you: "For once in my life, my words came out sure. . . . The inside peace that came from gazing at the baby. 'I know where the baby is. Follow me.'" How do you spend time gazing at the Christ Child? In inner meditation? In eucharistic adoration? In frequent, even daily, prayer?

Walking in the New Evangelization
by Kelly Wahlquist

As we conclude this chapter, think about how each aspect has spoken to your heart. What have the scriptures revealed to you? Which qualities of the women in the story resonated with you? How have your eyes been opened to walking in charity? Here are a couple of ways you can continue to reflect upon what you have discovered and grow in virtue.

Virtue in Action

Charity is loving God for his own sake above all things and loving our neighbor as ourselves. The fruits of charity are joy, peace, and mercy. We can receive these fruits and give them to others. It's a beautiful circle, for in giving to others, we receive—growing in the virtue of charity.

Make the time to go to eucharistic adoration. Gaze upon Jesus with love. Bring to him the needs of another, someone who is sick, homeless, imprisoned, dying, or lonely. Write a spiritual bouquet—a letter or card assuring that person of your prayers for them as you sit adoring Jesus, the Christ Child. Send it to that person (maybe anonymously) and look for opportunities to continue this adoration charity in the future.

Until next time . . . O Come, Let Us Adore Him!

4.

Gaze with Reverence
(The Presentation)

A Moment to Ponder
by Kelly Wahlquist

The Protoevangelium of James is a second-century document that offers us glimpses into the early life of the Holy Family that cannot be found in scripture yet which attest to ancient traditions regarding the names of Mary's parents and the story of Mary's dedication to the Lord as a young child:

> And [when] the child was three years old, Joachim said: Invite the daughters of the Hebrews that are undefiled, and let them take each a lamp, and let them stand with the lamps burning, that the child may not turn back, and her heart be captivated from the temple of the Lord. And they did so until they went up into the temple of the Lord. And the priest received her, and kissed her, and blessed her, saying: The Lord has magnified your name in all generations. In you, on the last of the days, the Lord will manifest his redemption to the sons of Israel. And he set her down upon the third step of the altar, and the Lord God sent grace upon her; and she

danced with her feet, and all the house of Israel loved
her.

And her parents went down marveling, and praising the Lord God, because the child had not turned
back. And Mary was in the temple of the Lord as if she
were a dove that dwelt there, and she received food
from the hand of an angel.[1]

Although she is not mentioned in this text, the timeline
of events suggests that Anna, the prophetess mentioned in
Luke, must have been worshiping in the Temple around
this time, entrenched in widowhood and listening for the
voice of the Spirit—the same Spirit who would one day
hover over Mary, causing her to bear the Hope of all Israel.

When she spotted Mary in the Temple with a baby in
her arms, did Anna feel a faint flush of recognition? Did her
heart rejoice at the sight of this beloved girl, now grown and
a mother herself? Did she look into the face of Mary's child
and recognize the depth of his expression? Did she savor
that moment, her reward for a lifetime of service?

Imagine for a moment how Mary might have felt, coming up the Temple steps and seeing this reminder of her
childhood. As the Law required, she was presenting herself for ritual purification following childbirth. She was no
longer a carefree girl but a grown woman with a husband
and child. Every fiber of her being was given over to this
new and all-consuming responsibility—the enormity of
which was compounded as she encountered first Simeon,
then Anna herself.

As you approach the Lord to receive him in the Eucharist, do you ever pause to present yourself to him, just as
you are? The Church teaches that those who commit serious
sin must go to Confession before receiving Communion,
but did you know that the Eucharist purifies us from venial
sins and breaks disordered attachments, helping us to avoid
future sins as well (see *CCC*, 1394)?

Just as Mary and Joseph presented their son to God with great reverence and thanksgiving, so we must present ourselves with thankful and reverent hearts. In this chapter, we will examine the connection between the Presentation and the virtue of reverence. As you read, take a few moments to prepare yourself for your next encounter with Christ in his eucharistic presence. *God, help us to turn toward you with hearts full of reverent thanksgiving—focused not upon our own needs and expectations but on the gift of this present moment. Let us lift our eyes . . . and listen for the approach of the Spirit.*

Enter the Scripture
by Sarah Christmyer

Read Luke 2:21–40 before you start.

At four weeks old, many babies lift and turn their heads. They start to make eye contact and track things that move in front of them. By six weeks of age, at least half of all babies recognize their parents and prefer them to strangers. Sometimes they'll smile or kick with pleasure when Mom or Dad comes into view.

It was at this stage, about six weeks after Jesus' birth, that Joseph and Mary take him to the Temple in Jerusalem, "to present him to the Lord" (Lk 2:22).

Just think: Jesus, the God-man, is presented to God the Father by his earthly father and mother in the place that for centuries has been *the* place of meeting, where God is present to his people. Christ is no longer the stiffly swaddled, sleeping infant who was looked at by shepherds. He is a baby who can see and recognize and respond.

Interestingly, this event that we in the Roman Catholic Church call the Presentation of the Lord, or sometimes the Purification of Mary, is called in the Byzantine tradition *The*

Encounter. I like that. There's the encounter of Mary and
Jesus with Simeon and Anna. There's the encounter of the
Law obeyed and the Spirit followed. There's the encounter
of the old Temple with the new, true Temple, Christ. So
much is coming together in this scene!

Pope Benedict XVI put it this way: "This is the meeting
point of the two Testaments, Old and New. Jesus enters the
ancient Temple; he who is the new Temple of God: he comes
to visit his people, thus bringing to fulfillment obedience to
the Law and ushering in the last times of salvation."[2]

Mary and Joseph take Jesus to the Temple for two reasons: to carry out Mary's ritual purification forty days after
childbirth and to present Jesus, her firstborn son, to God.[3]
For purification, to restore ritual purity after childbirth, a
mother was to offer a lamb for a burnt offering and a bird
for a sin offering (see Leviticus 12:1–8). If the price of a lamb
was beyond her means, a pair of pigeons or turtledoves
could be sacrificed instead.

Why was this necessary? Ever since their liberation
from Egypt, God's people were required to dedicate every
firstborn son to the Lord. In the original Passover, those
families who smeared the blood of Passover lambs on their
doorposts were spared the plague of death that fell on the
firstborn sons of Egypt. From then on, all firstborn children
of Israel belonged in a special way to God. They could be
dedicated to him in service or "redeemed" with a modest
offering.

Bethlehem is only six miles from Jerusalem, so I imagine Joseph and Mary could have left their lodgings after
breakfast and been back the same day, if they had wanted.
On their way up, the Holy Family may have passed by
fields of sheep that were destined for the Temple as well,
as sacrificial lambs. Mary and Joseph, unable to afford a
lamb, offered birds instead (see Luke 2:24). Only in retrospect can we see the irony—that by presenting Jesus at

the Temple, they *did* offer a spotless lamb, whose sacrifice would redeem the whole world.

In the context of making that offering, Mary experienced what St. John Paul II taught in *Redemptoris Mater* was "like a second Annunciation" (16). This time it's not an angel who comes to her but the "righteous and devout" Simeon, a man filled with the Holy Spirit and longing for "the consolation of Israel" (Lk 2:25). The Spirit had revealed to him that he would see the Messiah before he died. And the Spirit had moved him to enter the Temple that day and led him to the child.

What was that encounter like, do you think? Simeon gathered the six-week-old Jesus up in his arms and no doubt searched his face. Did Jesus hold his gaze? Did he kick and coo, as babies do, with recognition? The Lord is meeting his people, in the place of meeting, in the person of Simeon! "Mine eyes have seen thy salvation," Simeon proclaimed, "a light for revelation to the Gentiles, and for glory to thy people Israel" (Lk 2:30, 32).

Simeon's words evoke the prophet Isaiah's words of consolation to God's people in exile, telling them of the servant God will send to Israel and the nations (see Isaiah 42:6; 49:6).

Simeon's words also echo and confirm the angel's joyful message to Mary, and she and Joseph marvel at what he says. But as Simeon turns his attention to the mother of Jesus, a shadow falls on their encounter. That glorious light will be rejected. Simeon speaks of a fall and rising and of a sword that will pierce Mary's soul as well as her son's. Her *fiat* will be lived through suffering.

Grace and grief, glory and the Cross . . . they are inseparably linked from the start. It's something hidden deep in the mystery of God, that these opposites can coexist and be redemptive. And when they meet—in this encounter between Mary and Simeon, for example—what is to come of it? How should we react when we encounter truth in this light?

Anna, an elderly prophetess who fasted and prayed day and night in the Temple, comes on the scene "at that very hour" and shows us the way. Like the Old Testament prophetesses Miriam and Deborah before her,[4] she breaks out in thanks to God and tells everyone of his redemption. The one whom Simeon and she (and so many others before now) have spent a lifetime searching for has come.

Prayer

Lord, I want to see Jesus! Holy Spirit, inspire me. Help me recognize him when he is near and give him proper reverence.

Gaze Upon Jesus: Anna, the Prophetess

A story by Stephanie Landsem

Some of the priests called me a prophetess. Others called me aged or even addled.

Perhaps they were all right. Perhaps I was all those things. I knew only that I could have no other life but the one I lived in the Temple of the Lord. Praising him. Listening to the Spirit.

Each morning, for years beyond counting, I rose from my mat at the sound of the dawn trumpets and the opening of the great doors of the Temple. *Your face, oh Lord,* I prayed, *your face is what my heart seeks*. And each morning, for years beyond counting, the Spirit of the Lord settled in my soul like the warmth of the sun.

But today when I awoke, the Spirit didn't settle within me. Today the Spirit rushed and surged like the wind before a storm. Restless. Tumultuous.

What is it, Lord? I prayed.

But the Spirit did not answer.

As dawn broke through the rose-colored clouds, I wandered as if in a dream across the Court of the Gentiles. Wondering. Waiting. Listening.

I had lived in the Temple for decades. Indeed, since the death of my husband a lifetime ago, I had not left the Holy Place. And yet I felt as if I were seeing the Glory of Jerusalem for the first time.

On the east side of the immense court—among the morning shadows of the Royal Stoa—merchants set out cages holding turtledoves and pigeons and herded lambs into pens. Moneychangers dressed in rich robes adjusted their scales, their hands flashing with jeweled rings. A bevy of Alexandrians, bright as peacocks, exchanged their foreign coins for the Tyrian shekels needed to pay the Temple tax. A young man speaking in the heavy accent of Babylon looked over the lambs before pointing out his choice and handing over his coins.

I turned away from the merchants and stopped before the fifteen marble steps leading up to the Beautiful Gate, glittering like a newly lit fire in the first rays of the sun. I climbed the marble steps, my knees popping and my old hips creaking, and entered the Court of the Women. Slowly, I made my way to my place—the place I like to pray—in the eastern corner. Here, I watched the sun rise over the Mount of Olives and illuminate the deep green of the Kidron Valley far below. The scent of incense was familiar, but I felt untethered, as if seeking something . . . though I knew not what.

Something extraordinary.

I lifted my eyes past the Court of the Women to the glowing bronze doors of the Nicanor gate, through which only men could go. Up even further I gazed, past the Court of the Priests and the great altar of unhewn stone where the sacrifices were made. All the way up to the Holy of Holies, the highest pediment. My eyes rested upon the cedar door covered in gold—open, but draped with a magnificent embroidered veil. The dwelling place of the Lord.

Speak, I begged the Spirit. *Your servant is listening.*

I heard only the murmur of prayers and the shuffle of sandals on stone, but I was not troubled. When the Spirit willed it, I would hear his voice.

The cool breeze of morning lifted my head covering and teased wisps of snow-white hair over my eyes as my heart pondered with a bright new watchfulness I didn't understand. I had known both joy and sorrow in the years the Lord had given me. The joy of my wedding day and the love of a righteous man. A daughter who was the treasure of my heart. I'd seen my husband die of fever when we were both still young, and I'd outlived my daughter by more than fifty years. Yet each day, their faces come to me as clearly as if I'd kissed their cheeks yesterday. Their voices sound in my ears like the murmur of the wind through the trees.

Bountiful joy. Staggering sorrow. I had known both and thanked the Lord. Without the joy, I would not know his infinite love. Without the sorrow, how could I know his unending faithfulness?

My Lord. My God. The One who knew me before all others. The One who never leaves me. *You, oh Lord, are my portion and my hope*, I prayed to the One who has never left my heart. *Your mercies never cease; they are renewed each morning, so great is your faithfulness to your servant.*

Following the routine of my many years, I gathered the scraps of bread left behind by the Temple priests and brought them to the beggars sitting along the wall. Some days I shared their meager meal, but today I would fast as I waited for the Spirit to speak.

As the Women's Court began to fill with pilgrims, I swept the bird droppings and bits of straw scattered on the mosaic floor and polished the thirteen golden trumpets that received the thank offerings of the people. Not far from me, a woman pressed a silver coin into a blind man's hand. She was recently widowed, I knew, and had little to give. *Those who give to the poor will lack nothing, Lord.* A moment later, a group of Pharisees parted the crowd, their plump tassels brushing the floor and their heavy phylacteries swaying from linen headdresses. They barely glanced at the crippled beggars. *But those who close their eyes to poverty will be cursed.*

Both the righteous and the hypocrites abounded in the Temple of the Lord: pilgrims who braved the treacherous sea and scorching desert to praise him in the Holy City; rabbis who handed down the wise words of the prophets and sages. But the Temple also housed merchants who would cheat the poor for the price of a turtledove and Pharisees who performed pious acts but had no room for the Spirit in their hearts. *Those with ears to hear, hear the Lord. Those with eyes to see, see his faithfulness.* Even here in the Holy Courts, there were many who were deaf and blind.

My tasks done, I stopped to turn my soul to the Spirit, raising my face once again to the Holy of Holies. *I listen for your word, my God.*

This time, the Spirit was not silent. *Look,* the word of the Lord came. *Look and you will see.* I lowered my eyes and found the face of an old friend before me. Simeon. Here at the Temple. I stood like a statue, unable to draw a breath, as understanding dawned like the morning. Could it be? It had been many months—perhaps years—since Simeon had come to the Temple. Indeed, I wondered each day if I would hear that he'd left this world. But the prophecy . . . the one he said kept his soul alive . . . could the prophecy have brought him here today? Could that be the reason for my unrest?

Simeon's hands shook with palsy, yet he grasped at mine and didn't waste time with greetings. "Anna. Do you feel it?"

I nodded, my heart jumping to my throat. I took his arm and walked him to the shade of the portico. Simeon leaned on me, his body like a fragile bird, his skin stretched tight over sharp bones.

He lifted his cloudy eyes to mine. "He is here."

I did not ask him whom he meant. There was only one. Long ago, the Spirit had spoken to Simeon, had told him he would not see death before his eyes beheld the Messiah. Some doubted his words, but I believed him. Of course I believed him—he heard the same Spirit that spoke to me. I jerked my head up and surveyed the courtyard. How would the Messiah come? As a pillar of fire that protected our ancestors from the Egyptians? Or in a blazing chariot like the one that came for Elijah? Would he be a king with an army of angels who would cut down the Romans and restore Jerusalem to her people?

Yet the Court of the Women was as always.

We stood together in the shade. Watching. Praying. Listening.

I spoke again to the light of my soul. *Thank you, Lord, for your goodness. That I may live to see the redemption of your people, Israel.*

When the sun reached its zenith and the horns of sacrifice blew five times, I saw them. They stood inside the gate, a young woman holding an infant. A man, not young at all, holding a basket with two turtledoves. The daylight seemed to dim, or perhaps the light around the family was brighter, as if the reflection of the sun from the Holy of Holies shone down on them alone.

Could it be? A child? An infant, the Redeemer of Israel? My old heart fluttered, and I was drawn to them like a deer to running water.

Yes, whispered the Spirit.

And it was so. The Messiah had come. As an infant. A baby at his mother's breast. *How great, oh Lord, is your wisdom. How surprising are your works.*

Simeon lurched beside me, toward the family. I helped him across the court until we came to the foot of the bronze Nicanor gate. Simeon stepped in front of them and held out his shaking hands.

He wanted the baby.

The woman looked at her husband, and he nodded. Then she laid the bundled child carefully in Simeon's arms.

I'd seen enough mothers bring in their sin-offerings to know this was a male child, just over a month old. A daughter would be older, twice a son's age. The infant's eyes were open and rested on Simeon. They gazed at each other, one so recently brought into this world, the other soon to leave it. Simeon straightened, as if he were a strong young man again. I felt it, too. A power, like that of lightning or thunder in the sky.

It was the Spirit. No longer behind the purple curtain and contained within the golden Tabernacle, but here, hovering and surging.

I leaned over the babe. *Your face, oh Lord, is what my heart seeks.*

The babe turned his gaze on me. The one we awaited for centuries. The one all of Israel longed for. The savior of Israel had come not as a warrior or king . . . but as a babe. The Lord of Hosts was indeed unfathomable. *What glory is yours, Lord, to reveal yourself to us in a child.*

We stood—the old man with the babe, the mother and father, and me—embraced by the Spirit. Marveling. Pondering.

And then, as suddenly as it had come, the Spirit was gone.

Simeon swayed. I stepped forward to steady him as he bowed his head over the child. "Lord, now lettest thou thy servant depart in peace," his voice wavered, "for my eyes have seen thy salvation, which thou hast prepared in the presence of all peoples, a light for revelation to the Gentiles, and for glory to thy people Israel."

My heart swelled as if to burst. The revelation to the Gentiles, the Glory of Israel. *Give thanks to the Lord, for he is good. His mercy is for ages to come!*

Simeon went on, tears streaming down the crevices of his cheeks. "Behold, this child is set for the fall and rising of many in Israel, and for a sign that is spoken against." He stepped closer to the mother, and I supported him as he leaned close, his dry wrinkled hand clutched hers. "And you, blessed one, a sword will pierce through your own soul also, that thoughts out of many hearts may be revealed."

The young mother's brow creased.

Even in my joy, I heard the prophecy of sorrow. Yes, I knew. Joy and sorrow were the contradictions of the Lord. I bent closer to the mother and raised a hand to touch the soft swell of her cheek. So young. The Lord had entrusted to her care for the one who would save his people. The joy, I could hardly imagine. The sorrow, it would come like a sword, as Simeon had foretold. Joy and sorrow. *Thank you, oh Lord, for both.*

The Lord of Hosts would be faithful to her. She would not be alone. "You marvel at these words," I said, "but do not fear them. Hold them in your heart and ponder them in the years to come. The Spirit is with you now and will be with you later, holding you up at the hour of your greatest sorrow."

The young woman seemed to understand. She took the child in her arms and pulled him close. When they left us, I helped Simeon to the shade where he slumped as if he'd come to the end of a long race. His hand went slack in mine, "I have seen," he said softly. "It is finished." Simeon would not come to the Temple again, I knew. He had believed the word spoken to him by the Lord and seen his reward.

I raised my eyes to the golden Tabernacle. Was it also my time to go in peace?

No. The answer came as the Spirit swelled within me. I felt like a young girl again. I wanted to bound up the steps of the Court of the Women like a gazelle, instead of an old donkey like I was, singing of the Lord's goodness. I might be called addled or touched in the head. I might be called a prophetess. It did not matter.

I would proclaim the word of the Spirit to all who had ears to hear and eyes to see.

I had lived my life in hope of this day. I would live what time I had left—be it a year or a day or an hour—telling all who would listen that the messiah, the anointed, the savior of Israel had come to his people . . . at last.

In Search of Reverence: The Presentation
by Maria Morera Johnson

In his review of the book Learning the Virtues That Lead You to God, *Randall Smith explained what Fr. Romano Guardini taught of the virtue of reverence, in which we look not merely inward, but upward—attending to the order of reality that "transcends the immediate passions and needs of the moment."[5]*

"All true culture," wrote Fr. Guardini, "begins with the fact that man steps back. That he does not obtrude himself and seize hold of things, but leaves a space, so that there may be a place in which the person in his dignity, the work in its beauty, and nature in its symbolic power may be clearly discerned."[6] —Kelly Wahlquist

In this chapter on the Presentation, we see how Mary and Joseph fulfill the tenets of their faith by presenting the infant Jesus at the Temple and restore ritual purity from childbirth by offering a pair of turtledoves or two young pigeons (see Luke 2:24). Walking all those miles with an infant so soon after giving birth must have been particularly hard on Mary, yet she does not complain, for by honoring the tenets of her faith, she once more willingly surrenders her own will to the will of the One who had called her to become the mother of his Son. One more yes in a lifetime of unconditional assent that she felt at the core of her being, even now.

As a young woman, I thought I had a personal faith—something private that I had no real motivation to share. Working in secular environments certainly ingrained that idea in me, although I now recognize the error. It wasn't so much that I was unwilling to share my faith; it simply never occurred to me. I had never experienced the joy of being surrounded by a community of faithful.

It wasn't until I was well into my forties that I experienced what it was like to be by like-minded people—people who were in love with the Lord. It was then that I learned the importance of spiritual friendship, and as the story goes, my life hasn't been the same since. I still value the other friendships forged from common ground in rich life experiences, but living in spiritual sisterhood (and brotherhood) has been instrumental in strengthening my faith.

Without this sense of "home," of belonging, I went through life for years with a tepid faith that yielded little fruit. And yet, this was not the end of the story. Though I may have forgotten about God, God never forgot me.

The *Catechism of the Catholic Church* tells us, "Although man can forget God or reject him, He never ceases to call every man to seek him, so as to find life and happiness. But this search for God demands of man every effort of intellect, a sound will, 'an upright heart,' as well as the witness of others who teach him to seek God" (CCC, 30).

This witness of others is found in the tapestry of our faith, the Body of Christ, particularly in our parish communities. It is where we live our faith together. We worship as one in the celebration of the Holy Mass. We participate, together, in the sacrament of the Eucharist. We serve as witnesses in the sacraments of Baptism, Confirmation, Matrimony, Holy Orders, and the Anointing of the Sick. Even in the sacrament of Reconciliation, although it is celebrated privately, we are encouraged and strengthened by our brothers and sisters who, like us, are sinners and seek forgiveness.

Why? Why do we seek the Lord? And why do we seek the Lord in community, where "the witness of others" encourages, models, and teaches us how to worship, how to be reverent before our God? The *Catechism* continues:

> You are great, O Lord, and greatly to be praised: great is your power and your wisdom is without measure. And man, so small a part of your creation, wants to praise you: this man, though clothed with mortality and bearing the evidence of sin and the proof that you withstand the proud. Despite everything, man, though but a small a part of your creation, wants to praise you. You yourself encourage him to delight in your praise, for you have made us for yourself, and our heart is restless until it rests in you. (CCC, 30)

Consider the following as you think about the virtue of reverence and how you have been cultivating it in your own life:

- What do you think of when you hear the word "reverence"? Is reverence primarily a matter of the heart or of the way we present ourselves to the Lord? What is the basis for this belief?

- Why does the Bible so often speak of the "fear of the Lord" as the beginning of wisdom? (see Proverbs 9:10.) How do we see this illustrated in the story of the Presentation?

Reflect on the Meaning: The Presentation
by Mary Healy

In the little chapel where I used to attend Mass, I could count on seeing them every day: a young man with his two sons, ages about two and four. During the time of praise and worship before Mass, the father would sometimes kneel down with his face to the floor. With a sidelong glance, his two little boys would immediately follow suit. During Mass, at the Consecration, the three of them would again kneel before the Lord, their faces to the floor. The sight was indelibly impressed on me as an image of a father teaching his sons reverence for the Lord. Through his example, those two boys learned to recognize the hidden presence of the Lord and to respond to him with love and devotion.

Reverence is an attitude that allows you to see with the eyes of the heart what is invisible to earthly sight. It is the inner vision that perceives the unseen God and responds to him rightly. The biblical account of the Presentation is full of such seeing beyond the visible.

The prophets had foretold the day when the Lord would come to his temple. It would be a day of judgment and of purification. "The Lord whom you seek will suddenly come to his temple. . . . behold, he is coming, says the LORD of hosts. But who can endure the day of his coming, and who can stand when he appears? For he is like a refiner's fire and like fullers' soap; he will sit as a refiner and purifier of silver, and he will purify the sons of Levi" (Mal 3:1–3).

It would have been reasonable, then, to expect the Lord to come as a fierce warrior-king or a formidable judge. It is no wonder that when Mary and Joseph entered the Temple with the infant Jesus, hardly any of the thousands of people there had any idea of the drama of salvation that was unfolding in their midst. Who could ever have imagined that when the Lord came to his temple, he would come as a *baby*? Can anything be more vulnerable and nonthreatening than a baby? What more could God do to show his desire to draw near to us, his yearning for our love?

Mary and Joseph were among the poor of Israel. The best their resources could produce for an offering to God was a pair of cheap birds. Yet ironically, God himself gave them something of infinite value to offer: God's own Son. In their poverty, they offered God to God! What reverence must have moved them as they presented before the Lord that most weighty treasure, costlier than all the galaxies in the cosmos. And we do the same at every Mass: we offer our poverty—our limited resources, our feeble virtues, our failures, and our sins—along with the incalculably valuable gift of God's own Son. And our offering becomes priceless!

Mary and Joseph were not dismayed by the fact that they could only offer what they had received as a gift. They knew the Lord was pleased beyond measure with their giving it back to him. They saw into the mystery of God's love: although he needs nothing, he desires our love in return for his love.

Simeon and Anna too saw beyond the visible. As true Israelites, they had spent their lives in reverent hope for the Messiah, clinging to God's promises. "I wait for the LORD, my soul waits, and in his word I hope; my soul waits for the LORD more than watchmen for the morning" (Ps 130:5–6). Their reverence had given them x-ray vision. There must have been dozens of couples entering the Temple that day to present their firstborn sons. There was no visible halo, no royal splendor to mark Mary and Joseph's child as unique. Yet Simeon and Anna had the "eyes of [their] hearts enlightened" (Eph 1:18) to look into the eyes of a six-week-old baby and see the face of God.

The Lord hid himself astoundingly in the infant Jesus and even more astoundingly in Jesus nailed to the Cross. But he hides himself in many ways—especially, as Mother Teresa used to say, "in the distressing disguise of the poor." Reverence is needed to see the Lord seeking our love and attention in his hidden ways.

One time I was with a few friends visiting the Solanus Casey Center in Detroit, Michigan, honoring this Franciscan priest who, as the monastery doorkeeper, had humbly welcomed and served many thousands of people. As we left the center and were going back to our car, a panhandler across the street called out to us, asking for a handout. Another man who had just exited the center advised us, "Just get into your car quickly." Three of us did, but my friend Katie immediately walked across the street and began talking to the grungy panhandler. She said, "I don't have any money to give you, but would you like a prayer?" His face immediately broke into a grin and without a moment's hesitation he knelt down on the sidewalk, and she prayed over him. I was convicted with how easily I had let earthly vision dominate and had missed an opportunity to reverence and serve the Lord in the least of his brethren.

After their encounter with Jesus, Simeon and Anna each responded in their own way to the extraordinary grace they had received. Simeon knew his life's mission had been fulfilled, and he was ready to go home to the Lord. Anna, on the other hand, realized that at age eighty-four, her mission was by no means over! She was called to make known the hidden God. So this woman whose whole life had been dedicated to prayer, fasting, and worship now became an evangelist. "She gave thanks to God, and spoke of him to all who were looking for the redemption of Jerusalem" (Lk 2:38). This too is part of reverence: to make known to those who do not yet see the presence of the hidden God in our midst.

- What is most often the reason you tell yourself that God couldn't possibly be calling you to present yourself or to embark on a mission for him? Are you too old, busy, or uneducated? How does the story of Anna speak to you?

- Bl. Solanus Casey, like Simeon and Anna, spent a good deal of his life in prayer and humble service. When people came to him with their most pressing needs, he would instruct them merely to "thank God ahead of time" for the answer to their prayers. In the Presentation, we are reminded that the answer does not always come quickly but that God is always faithful to answer. How have you seen this to be true in your life?

Visio Divina: Contemplate the Lord through Sacred Images
by Dr. Elizabeth Lev and Kelly Wahlquist

Raphael (Raffaello Sanzio), *Presentation in the Temple*,
1505. Photo © Vatican Museums. All rights reserved.

The image for this *visio divina* exercise is called *Presentation in the Temple*, by Raphael (Raffaello Sanzio da Urbino, 1505). The original hangs in the Vatican Museums' Pinacoteca (Painting Gallery) in Rome.

Raphael was nineteen years old when he worked on this scene, which is part of a prestigious altarpiece. His mastery of both perspective and composition draws the onlooker into the narrative. His use of soft shadows to outline figures, derived from his study of the work of Leonardo da Vinci, introduced a serenity and harmonious quality that made Raphael's style a universally popular form of visual communication.

Find the color image of Raphael's *Presentation in the Temple* at the front of the book. Spend a few moments gazing on it before returning to the reflection. Use a bookmark to hold your place so you can return to it easily.

Focus your attention on the characters in the painting, noticing their expressions and movements, and the colors, spaces, and shapes that surround them. Ask the Holy Spirit to help you look with the eyes of a prayerful wonderer and contemplate what you see.

A symmetrical spacing of columns, colors, and people creates a unified and orderly backdrop for a dramatic moment in history—God Incarnate is present in the Temple. Focus your gaze on Jesus and contemplate the objects and the actions of the people around him.

In the center of the painting beneath the Bread of Life is a wooden fixture that resembles the ciborium, which holds consecrated hosts. As the eyes of the three central people are tenderly looking at the Infant Jesus, a story is playing out: the baby is reaching for the comfort of his mother's embrace.

As you gaze upon this two-dimensional painting, notice how the people, dressed in robes that suggest nobility, appear to be moving with dignity and grace. Their individual facial expressions portray a sense of calm and serenity, as if they are engaged in normal everyday conversations, totally unaware of the true Royalty before them. How often does that happen to you? Do you get so tied up in the circumstances of daily life that you miss the presence of Jesus? Take a moment to ask Jesus to open the eyes of your heart to his presence.

Notice too that the buildings and clothing styles are not that of the time of Jesus. Perhaps Raphael is reminding us that God can and does meet us wherever we are on this journey. Close your eyes, open your heart and say to the Lord, "Jesus, enlighten the eyes of my heart; allow me to understand how much you yearn for me to know and love you. Help me to recognize your presence in the everyday occurrences in my life, and guide me to make your presence known to those who do not see you hidden in our midst."

Questions for Group Discussion
by Dr. Carol Younger

Below are questions from various sections of the chapter to help each member of the small group grow in knowledge and faith.
—Kelly Wahlquist

1. Encounter! That person-to-person meeting shining with emotion and meaning. Have you encountered Jesus? Perhaps you were carried as a baby to holy waters of life in Christ, but have you encountered him? Has there been a time in your life where you encountered his mercy? A time when you were overcome by his love for you? Do you remember a moment when you were joy-fully surprised by the encounter with Christ? Was it in a Bible study? In the witness of a person who knew Jesus intimately? In the action of one who cared for another? Share some thoughts about your first encounter with Jesus, when you knew you would forever belong to him and longed to see his face (see Psalm 42).

2. Anna sees the significance of Simeon's prophecy, the Law and the prophets present in person, and cannot contain her joy. How do you display your joy in Jesus? Do you say a good morning or a hello to those who pass your way, adding a "God bless you"? Do you share your smile with those you meet, inviting them to stop

to talk? When you are asked for your prayers, how do you respond? Share a time when you were able to tell someone about your joy in Jesus.

3. Psalm 42:2 states, "My soul thirsts for God, for the living God. When shall I come and behold the face of God?" Anna rises every day in the same hope and reverence for God's Temple. Perhaps you also arise with prayer and faithful thanksgiving each day. You *yourself* are the Temple where he comes to present himself to you. You can see him each day in his Word. You can invite him in Holy Communion every day to reside in your temple. Choose a psalm or a story from the Old or New Testament; read it aloud and let him speak to you. Share with your group what he said to you in this encounter with his Word.

4. Have you ever heard the whisper of the Spirit announce a response to a question your heart asks? Anna asks if it is her time to be dismissed as Simeon is. "No" is the immediate answer. Share a time when the Spirit spoke to you in prayer. What did you hear? What were your feelings then? How did you respond? Were you prompted to proclaim his great love, mercy, and salvation? Who do you believe needs to hear it first?

Walking in the New Evangelization
by Kelly Wahlquist

As we conclude this chapter, think about how each aspect has spoken to your heart. What have the scriptures revealed to you? Which qualities of the women in the story resonated with you? How have your eyes been opened to walking in reverence? Here are a couple of ways you can continue to reflect upon what you have discovered and grow in virtue.

Virtue in Action

Contemplating our own sacred moments of awe, encountering his presence, always draws us closer to God. This week, be consciously in awe of God. Make an effort to see God in all things, in all of his creations and all of his creatures—in the homeless, the poor, even in those who cut you off in traffic. React as though each person is the hidden Jesus: react with your heart. Either in the moment or at the end of each day, close your eyes, let the wonder fill you, and contemplate the beauty of his creation—and the goodness of every creature and the God who made them.

Until next time, make a special effort to reverence the Lord when you become conscious of his presence.

5.

Gaze with Courage
(The Flight to Egypt)

A Moment to Ponder
by Kelly Wahlquist

The prophet Hosea, who lived in the eighth century BC, is perhaps best known for marrying the prostitute Gomer, whose subsequent infidelities mirrored the faithlessness of the Israelites, to whom God had sent Hosea just before the destruction of Israel in 722 BC. Chapter after chapter in the book of Hosea, the prophet denounces the faithless Israel and predicts its downfall. And yet, even in this, God is faithful not to entirely extinguish their hope.

> When Israel was a child, I loved him,
> and out of Egypt I called my son.
> The more I called them,
> the more they went from me; . . .
> I led them with cords of compassion,
> with the bands of love. (Hos 11:1–2, 4)

From the nineteenth century BC, when Jacob and his family took up residence in Egypt after their son Joseph rose to power (see Genesis 46–47), to the rise of Moses and the Exodus four centuries later (see Exodus 12–14), another seven hundred years pass before Israel is destroyed by Assyria.[1] It is seven hundred years after this that the promised Messiah, who restores the kingdom of God, arises— just as Israel once had—to free his people not just from the grip of the Romans but from much greater enemies—sin, Satan, and death.

This liberty, however, was not without cost. It required faith and fortitude, from the moments the angel stood before Mary, telling her she had been chosen to bear the Son of God, and before Joseph, commanding him to take Mary as his wife, until—as parents of the only infant to escape the wrath of Herod—they fled the only life they'd ever known to return once more to the land their people had always associated with bondage, plagues, and death. Think of the courage it must have taken!

As you read this chapter, think of this dark chapter in the life of the Holy Family, when they were strangers in a strange land. They needed great courage and clear-eyed hope. Can you relate to this in your own life? When you sense God is calling you to "flee," does it take greater courage to go . . . or to stay?

Enter the Scripture
by Sarah Christmyer

Read Matthew 2:1–23 before you start.

"Wise men still seek him," as the saying goes.

Wise women, too, I think, as I place camels and the three Magi along the mantelpiece. At the start of Advent, I cluster these together at one end, far from the manger and the star. Every week I move them closer, and I think about that journey. I, too, follow the star that shines above the Lord. I, too, long to see his face.

There's something wonderful about a group of "wise men from the East" (Mt 2:1) following the light of a star to the light of Christ. The word translated as "wise men" or "magi" (Greek *magoi*) has several meanings, from Zoroastrian priests to astronomers and magicians. The Magi became popularly known as "kings" after early Christians read Matthew's gospel in light of Old Testament prophecies that all kings and nations will fall down and worship the Messiah.[2] Whoever these Magi actually were, they were Gentiles who knew Jesus only as "king of the Jews." They were wise men on a mission, seeking . . . what? The Star of Bethlehem marked Jesus as a very special king. He was worthy of worship even at the cost of a long journey.

From their actions, it is evident that these visiting dignitaries see Jesus as a king, despite his reduced circumstances. They prostrate themselves in worship and give gifts more suited to a king than to a carpenter's son: precious and valuable *gold*, symbolizing kingship; the aromatic resin *frankincense*, which was burned in the Temple and which symbolized the Divine Name, thus deity (see Malachi 1:11); and *myrrh*: an embalming oil that symbolized death. Together they represent the one who is born to be king and who is both mortal and divine.

Our nativity sets show Magi approaching Jesus in the manger, but it is more probable that by the time these gifts are given, Jesus is more than forty days old (his age at the Presentation, after which they returned to Nazareth), and possibly a year older than that. Herod orders the death of all boys under the age of two, based on the appearance of the star. The Magi find "the child with Mary his mother" in "the house," not Mary and Joseph with a newborn among the animals (Mt 2:11). Art that places the Magi at the manger casts a rosy glow over the royal visit. It's easy to forget that this encounter is closely associated with slaughter and exile. Mary has already learned, from Simeon, that with this

child comes light and a sword. The light brings the Magi
. . . and the Magi, however unwittingly, attract the sword.

Matthew carefully tells all of these events in such a
way as to show how Jesus' early life fulfills Old Testament
scripture.

Born in Bethlehem

The birth in Bethlehem fulfills the prophecy that from Bethlehem "shall come a ruler who will govern my people Israel."[3] After returning from Egypt, his family's settling in
Nazareth fulfills another prophetic word: that "he shall be
called a Nazarene."[4]

Exiled in Egypt

The Holy Family's detour in Egypt comes about to fulfill
Hosea's prophetic word, "Out of Egypt have I called my
son."[5] Long before, God's "son," Israel, was enslaved in
Egypt. Moses grew up there and brought his people out of
Egypt in the Exodus. Now God's true Son, Jesus, is called
out of Egypt to achieve a definitive Exodus for all from the
power of sin.

Survived the Slaughter of Innocents

Herod's massacre of the male children around Bethlehem
fulfills Jeremiah, who spoke of "a voice in Ramah, . . . Rachel
weeping for her children . . . because they were no more."[6]
This matriarch of Israel died not far from Ramah, and her
tomb later was moved to Bethlehem. Jeremiah pictures her
grieving as her children (representing the tribes of Israel)
are killed and taken into exile.

To Matthew, this prophetic word prefigures the slaughter of children around Bethlehem and Jesus' exile to Egypt.
He may also have been recalling the Old Testament context:
through Jeremiah, the Lord tells Rachel—and Israel—to
stop weeping because they will one day return. Some do

return to the land, but true return from exile comes only through Jesus, who first enters into his people's grief.

Slaughter and exile and slavery are some of the worst things that can happen to a people. Together they represent what the devil strives to do to the children of God, both in Israel and today. He seeks to destroy them, to pull them away from God's presence, and to enslave them so they cannot worship. Jesus comes to save us all from this.

When I gaze on the Christ child at Bethlehem, leaving for Egypt, this is what I see: God coming to save us. For some unknown reason (unless it's so we feel his love), he doesn't simply wave the pain away. Rather, he plunges headlong into the mess right beside us. This small child, who is weak and helpless and poor just like we are, makes himself vulnerable to the plots and dangers of the world. Even as a child, he becomes present *in* our pain. Why? To transform it from the inside and defeat it forever.

Matthew doesn't give us details of Jesus' stay in Egypt. He's more focused on the dreams that allow us to see Joseph in light of the Joseph of Genesis, who had prophetic dreams and whose exile to Egypt saved Israel from famine. In both stories, God works through events that are meant for evil, to bring about good (see Genesis 50:20–21).

Coptic Christians remember this event not as Jesus' exile but as "Our Lord's Entry into Egypt." Their joyous feast celebrates Jesus going to Egypt to bless the land and its people, fulfilling Isaiah 19. Thus the edict that Herod intended to bring death to the Christ Child meant instead blessing to the Gentiles.

Prayer

Lord, I want to see Jesus! Even when following or carrying him takes me into danger, let me see your good. Help me gaze with courage on what Jesus means in my life.

Gaze Upon Jesus: Adrina, the Wife of Melchior

A story by Stephanie Landsem

I, Adrina, was the first wife of Melchior, priest of Persia, and the one he loved best.

Melchior was a trader of spices, and his tents were full of children and wives and slaves. But wives and children and spices are not what brought him joy. It was the truth of the stars that he desired above all else.

My husband belonged to the ancient caste of priests of Persia. Indeed, he was one of three considered most wise in Persepolis. Each night, Melchior, Gaspar, and Balthazar searched the skies for the one they called the unknown god. This god, they said, was one a man could approach without fear. A god who would send a king . . . a king of peace.

They had good hearts, these men of the sky, but they were blind. Melchior and his priests lived in the stars, while my own feet were planted firmly on this earth. For all gods were to be feared . . . and I had never known of a king who loved peace.

Each year, the priests were called to the court of Arsaces to prophesy. I advised Melchior to tell the king what he wanted to hear—for a king desires power, not truth—but of course he refused. I feared that one day his search for truth would lead us into danger.

And so it did.

It began as the cold shamal wind blew into our winter camp. For many nights, Melchior did not come to my bed, nor the beds of his other wives. Each morning saw him more drawn and serious. Finally, I sat him on my own silk cushion, brought him spiced wine, and rubbed his temples with sweet almond oil.

At last, he told me. "The star of Babylon and the star of Judah have risen and joined. They shine brighter than anything the night skies have ever seen."

I refilled his wine and wondered at his words.

My husband did not drink from his cup but took my hand in his. "The time has come, Adrina. The king of peace will come out of Judah, as the ancients foretold."

I felt the chill of foreboding. What did this king matter to us, here in a land so far from Judah? But I feared I knew.

He met my eyes. "I must go—with Balthazar and Gaspar—to find this king that the stars announce."

My blood ran cold in my veins. Into Judah? A land held by the Romans, as ruthless an empire as the world had ever seen? They would not welcome a king of peace. And Herod, the Numidian king of the Jews? Talk of his jealous cruelty had reached us for years. Any rival for Herod's throne was bound to lead to bloodshed. My husband thought little of danger, but I knew it when I saw it.

"I shall go with you." I said, although I feared neither of us would return.

And so we left Persepolis. We turned our backs to the home of Xerxes and the ancient palace of Darius and traveled for weeks across the desert. Three camels for Melchior, Gaspar, and Balthasar. Twenty more for me, our slaves, tents, and foodstuffs. Fifty armed men rode in front of our caravan and fifty behind. During the cold desert nights, we traveled by the light of the moon. In the heat of the day, we slept in the shade of our tents. Sand settled in my eyes, my fingers and toes; even my mouth was filled with the fine grit of the desert wind. We left on the cusp of winter, and arrived on the Plain of Sharon as spring scented the air with the fragrance of wet earth, newly planted fields, and the blossoms of the terebinth tree.

Perhaps we looked like an invading army, with our camels and guards, for we were met by an emissary from the tetrarch, braced with a host of armed soldiers that belied his gracious words. "My Lord Herod bids you welcome, and to feast with him at his palace."

I helped Melchior dress in his finest robe, a deep blue silk with gold cord and tiny silver bells. "Just a year ago, Herod ordered the death of his own sons for fear they desired his throne," I whispered, distress drying my throat.

"We seek only knowledge," he told me as if that would protect him.

With shaking hands, I donned my best gown and gathered gifts to appease a treacherous king.

Herod's emissary, who called himself Jabez and had the bearing of a soldier, led us into the city—Melchior, Gaspar, and Balthazar on camels and I in a litter carried by eight of my most trusted slaves. Jerusalem's streets were narrow and winding, teeming with Jews in tasseled robes and Greeks with curled beards. We passed a great temple that was indeed as glorious as any in Persia. White marble and gold, it soared into the blue Judean sky. The scent of incense and burnt animal flesh drifted on the breeze. This Hebrew god, I surmised, was like all the other gods I'd known—one of sacrifice and immolation.

The palace of the king of the Jews was almost as magnificent as the temple to their god. We left the camels and my litter at the massive arched entrance and climbed polished marble steps to a sprawling palace ringed with gardens, fountains, and groves of sweet eucalyptus.

"You will go to the women's rooms," Jabez told me with an unctuous bow and gave me to the charge of a slave who brought me through a hall of soaring ceilings and ebony doors. I entered a room filled with women in silk and linen, gold in their hair and on their wrists. Envious eyes roamed over my green silk robe and pleated sleeves embroidered with silver. My golden bangles and jeweled hair gave honor to my husband's wealth and the bounty of Persia and bolstered my own courage.

"Your husband is there," the slave nodded to an iron-work screen. I went close, peering through the filigree into a great feasting room. Men reclined on couches and sprawled on benches. Slave girls filled wine cups and musicians played the lyre and flutes. On a raised dais, an immense man reclined. His robes were the purple of royalty, but his skin the color of curdled milk. A slave stood by with a linen towel, wiping the sweat that streamed from his brow and the pus that leaked from his eyes and nose.

My heart sped up. Herod was, indeed, a king to fear.

Jabez announced the Magi of Persia, and the room quieted. My husband came before the throne, noble and dignified. Balthazar followed, splendid in his blue velvet miter, and then Gaspar, the oldest of the priests, with his long, white beard and jeweled staff. Melchior presented Herod with the gift—a casket of ebony crusted in pearls. Inside were precious beads of pepper, more costly than gold.

Herod waved the gift aside and rasped a command in a voice like a crow. "Men from the east, tell me what you seek."

My heart crept into my throat. I had cautioned my husband to guard his words. Talk of a king—even a king of peace—to a man like Herod would be unwise.

And yet, my husband was a man of truth, not of intrigue. "I have seen a star rise that foretells a newborn king of the Jews. My people and I come to do him homage."

I heard the sharp gasps of the women behind me. The feasting men and even the slaves went still.

A great and terrible silence filled the room as Herod struggled to pull his flaccid body upright. "A king of the Jews has been born?" he gasped out. "Jabez, bring me the priests."

It seemed like hours passed. I sipped strong, spiced wine but tasted only fear. A girl danced for the men, but Herod sat in silence, his cup filled many times over by a slave whose hand shook. Unease filled the air like the stench of death under sweet incense. Finally, a line of men processed into the room, strange-looking indeed. They wore white linen and had long beards. Their heads were wrapped, and small boxes dangled over their brows.

Herod struggled upright, and the slave wiped his sweating cheeks. "Tell me, where is this so-called king? And to whom has he been born?" Herod barked.

Silence fell like a sharp sword.

Finally, one priest stepped forward, licking his lips nervously. "You are the only king of the Jews, my Lord."

"Tell me of the child!" The tetrarch roared, brown spittle coming from his mouth.

The priest's throat jumped like a frog's. "The scriptures say only this," he recited. "'But you, O Bethlehem . . . from you shall come forth for me one who is to be ruler in Israel.'" His voice wavered as Herod's face turned crimson. "'He shall stand and feed his flock in the strength of the LORD. . . . He shall be great to the ends of the earth.'" The priest's voice died, and he stepped back as if to hide himself among the others.

Herod considered the priests with narrowed eyes, and then turned his gaze on Melchior. I tensed, ready to run, although I would not abandon my husband to Herod's wrath.

"Leave us." Herod finally said, his glance taking in the room. It emptied as quickly as a sinking boat. The women behind the screen were still, as if we all held our breath. My husband, Balthazar, and Gaspar approached the dais at Herod's beckoning finger. "When did this star appear?"

Balthazar answered. "At this time one year ago."

Herod leaned forward. "Go then, my friends, and search for this child." He appeared to be smiling but looked more like a cobra about to strike. "When you have found him, come back to me and tell me of him, that I too may go and do homage."

My husband bowed. Caspar and Balthazar did the same. "We will do as you command." They retreated backwards, the king of the Jews watching with red-rimmed eyes.

I did not breathe easy until we reached the litter and camels outside the palace. "He is mad," I whispered to my husband so that Jabez would not hear, for he was charged to remain with us.

But my husband seemed to have forgotten Herod already. "Bethlehem," he said, looking to south, "It is but five hundred people. We will search tomorrow."

A cold finger of fear brushed my spine. We would do better to leave this place as quickly as we had come. Not only for our sakes but for the sake of the child-king whom my husband sought.

As men find their answers in the sky, so women find theirs at the well. And that was how we found the child. A girl, lame and with a withered arm, answered my questions about a child born in Bethlehem who might be called a king. And so, Melchior, Balthazar, Gaspar, and I once again arrayed ourselves in splendor and gathered gifts. I charged one of my slave girls to keep Jabaz's attention, and so we left our camp without his vigilant presence.

The crippled girl led us to a place as unlike a king's palace as gold is to straw.

Where there had been marble and ebony in Herod's opulent court, here was a small house made of stone and clay. Instead of the costly perfumes, the fragrance of grass and dung in the tiny courtyard. And instead of priests and slaves, a man stooped with age and a woman with a child in her arms. The child was not yet two years old, with dark curling hair and curious eyes. The mother, whose name was Mary, and her husband, Joseph, were just as unremarkable. I could see no reason to believe that this child was a king, but my husband's faith in the stars had never been something I understood.

Melchior bowed low before the child. Balthazar and Gaspar went to their knees. "We have found him, the light of heaven." Gaspar proclaimed. They presented him with a cask of gold and alabaster jars of frankincense and myrrh—strange gifts indeed for a child but gifts my husband had carefully chosen.

Mary offered us hospitality. I joined her in serving bread and wine and figs.

Melchior did not take his eyes off the child. Gently, he asked Mary to tell him of this king of peace, as he called him. Mary told us of an angel who had come to her and the prophecy of her kinswoman who had been with child also. We learned of how she had given birth to the child in a cave not far from where we sat and heard a prophecy in the Temple when he was weeks old.

I marveled at the mother's story, yet I wondered. Surely this little boy could not be the son of a god. What kind of god would send a child against a king such as Herod? And from a simple family, with no heritage or power? The child, whom they had named Jesus, played with his mother's spindle as she talked, unfurling thread and trying to wind it back around the skein. He dropped it, and I bent to pick it up and put it back in his dimpled hand.

He smiled at me.

I thought of Herod's face as the priests told of the prophecy, and fear coursed through me. I might not believe this child was a king, but Herod would take no chance.

"They must leave here," I said to my husband when Mary went for more wine. "The child is in danger."

"It is not our task, nor our burden," he answered, shaking his head. "The unnamed god will protect them."

I had never questioned my husband before and would never defy him outright, but I left Bethlehem with a weight on my heart and the face of the child—his innocent smile—in my mind.

Jabez awaited us in camp, and his eyes narrowed as he took in our fine robes.

"Tomorrow, we return to Herod, as we promised." Melchior told Jabez.

Fear chilled my blood. When Jabez left us, I appealed to Balthazar and Gaspar. "It is too dangerous, is it not? We cannot anger a king such as Herod." But my husband's fellow priests agreed that they should do as promised. Was I the only one who could see the danger we would all face if we returned to Herod? And the danger to the child?

In the end, it was not my pleading that changed my husband's course but a dream. I woke in the dark of night to find our camp in an uproar. "Hurry," Melchior said, his face drawn and pale, "We must leave at once, and not for Jerusalem."

"What of Jabez?" I asked.

"He has gone to report our departure to Herod." Melchior rushed me to my mount. "We have no time to waste."

My heart sank. "What of the child?" I asked him. "Herod will find him. His parents . . ."

"We must do as the dream commanded." Melchior said, settling me on my camel. "His god will protect him."

I stared at my husband's back as he rode toward the front of the caravan. His god? What god deigns to protect a child of humble birth? I closed my eyes but still saw his innocent smile, his curious eyes. My husband may have trusted the god of Israel and believed in a dream, but I could not. Someone had to warn them. And so, for the first time in my life, I disobeyed my husband.

As Melchior led the caravan toward the desert, I dismounted and found my most loyal slave. "Wait here for me." If I slipped away on foot, Melchior would not notice my absence until well after the sun rose. I would be back by then, I hoped, and would make haste to rejoin the slow-moving caravan.

I hurried through the Kidron Valley. Bethlehem had seemed close when I traveled by litter, but now the dim flicker of the city walls looked distant. The star—the joining of Judah and Babylon that had pointed us to this land— outshone the sliver of moon. As I came within sight of the city wall, a flurry of light bloomed in the north, where the Valley of Gehenna sloped up to the Jerusalem wall.

Torches.

I froze, my heart leaping into my throat. I saw a host of men, and they were marching toward Bethlehem. I knew at once that they were coming for the child.

I ran. I reached the walls of Bethlehem and slipped through a side door near the gate. The slap of my sandals echoed through the quiet streets. I had to reach him in time. I had never prayed to the gods of Persia or any other, but that night I prayed for the first time in my life. *Can you hear me, O God of Israel? If you really are their god, save the child and his parents.*

I found the house on its narrow street. I had to wake them, to somehow convince them to flee. I burst through the courtyard gate. "Mary, Joseph! You must—"

But they were not asleep. Mary held the child, wrapped in a blanket. Joseph loaded a pack on a sleepy donkey.

They already knew. How did they? Who had come to them?

Joseph read my stunned expression. "A dream," Joseph said. "The Lord sent an angel to me in a dream. Herod is searching for the child, and we must go to Egypt."

"Yes," I affirmed, knowing that the soldiers might already have reached the walls of Bethlehem. "They are coming."

Mary put the child in my arms. He stirred, sleepy and warm. She helped Joseph fasten the packs, and then gathered rounds of bread and a skin of water. She was not afraid. How could she not be afraid? Did she have that much faith in her god's protection? And then I remembered her story of the angel's announcement, the birth of the child, the prophecy in the Temple.

Yes, she did.

I was astonished. I looked down at the child in my arms. He gazed sleepily back at me. Was it possible that this god of Israel was not a god to fear? Could this unnamed god truly love his people, as my husband claimed? Would he watch over them even now?

There was little time to marvel. I followed Joseph and Mary out of the courtyard and into the dark street.

I took one last look at the child and brushed a kiss over his dark curls; then I gave him back to his mother's waiting arms.

"Thank you for coming to us," Mary said simply, brushing her cheek against mine.

I had known them only hours, and yet as they disappeared into the dark shadows of the southern gate, my heart felt as if it had been pierced. "May your god go with you," I whispered.

Had their god heard my prayer? Would he save them as Melchior had foreseen?

A shouted command came from the west. The groan of the gate, the clatter of marching feet. The soldiers had come. I hurried back through the town as black clouds shrouded both the sliver of moon and the bright star, casting the streets in darkness. I heard soldiers pounding on doors. They were looking for the child. Only I knew where the child had gone, and I would never tell. I found the door through which I'd come and stumbled through it as a woman's cry split the darkness. I leaned against the wall, my heart turning in my chest. A child's wail, cut short. The clash of sword on stone.

What was happening?

I peered through the narrow opening and saw a grim-faced soldier carrying a child—an infant, unmoving, covered in blood. A keening mother went to her knees. And then I knew. My legs weakened and my stomach wrenched. Herod—deranged, power-mad Herod—had not sent his soldiers to kill the child Jesus. He'd sent them to kill every child in Bethlehem.

Tears wet my face as I ran. I ran from the dying children and the weeping women.

Herod was indeed a king to fear. A king with no mercy. A king of blood.

I prayed again to the unknown god. The god of Israel. I prayed that the child—the king of peace, as my wise husband called him—would someday return. That somehow, he would bring peace. To his people. To this land. Perhaps even to all people in every land.

If he was truly the son of a god, could anything be impossible?

I ran and I prayed and I did not look back.

In Search of Courage: The Flight into Egypt

by Maria Morera Johnson

Many of us have no clearer idea what we are capable of facing and enduring as when life hangs in the balance. Whether it is a grueling medical treatment, an untimely pregnancy, or the plight of a helpless creature who needs our help, it is the virtue of courage that helps us rise to the occasion . . . and, having risen, to persevere. The virtue of courage corresponds to the virtue of fortitude, one of the seven gifts of the Holy Spirit that is entrusted to each of us at Baptism and is infused in our souls at Confirmation (see Isaiah 11:2–3; Wisdom 8:7; CCC, 1808). This gift is what enables us to listen and respond to the voice of the Spirit—and the same Spirit that protected the Holy Family as they fled to Egypt can be trusted to guide the steps of anyone who commits her life to God, as we discover in this testimony. —Kelly Wahlquist

When I share my immigration story, people are often aghast at the trials and sacrifice my family suffered, even though my presence is a testament to a happy ending.

My story begins with my parents' hasty marriage. My father, who opposed the communist government, decided to emigrate. He obtained a legal exit from Cuba and a legal entry into the United States. He then asked my mother to join him, and my grandparents granted permission if they were first married. He left shortly after they were married to begin the reclamation process for my mother and get a job and an apartment for her arrival. Unbeknownst to them, she was pregnant with me when he left.

Every month, my father received a rejection letter from the State Department. Every month, my mother prepared a little more for my arrival into the world, worried I would never know my father. After I was born, three more years passed before my mother and I received our visas, my parents were reunited, and I met my father.

When I think of courage, I don't have to look past my own mother. She exemplified the virtue in ways I still cannot grasp. My mother maintained a deep devotion and commitment to my father and their wedding vows when others, defeated, quietly got divorces and started new lives. She maintained her faith and endeavored to raise me Catholic within a communist regime that had declared war on religion. Within it all, she strove to instill in me the knowledge that my father loved us and his absence was circumstantial. One day we would be together again.

I believe my mother's strength, her fortitude in the face of this long separation, was aided by the theological virtue of hope. Hope gave wings to her courage. The *Catechism of the Catholic Church* defines this kind of hopeful courage as *fortitude*.

> *Fortitude* is the moral virtue that ensures firmness in difficulties and constancy in the pursuit of the good. It strengthens the resolve to resist temptations and to overcome obstacles in the moral life. The virtue of fortitude enables one to conquer fear, even fear of death, and to face trials and persecutions. It disposes one even to renounce and sacrifice his life in defense of a just cause. "The Lord is my strength and my song" [Psalm 118:14]. "In the world you have tribulation; but be of good cheer, I have overcome the world" [John 16:33]. (CCC, 1808)

As a woman, I can imagine the fear and hopelessness that my mother might have experienced. I've raised children with the help of a loving husband—I cannot fathom doing it alone, even though many women do. Yet my mother remained disposed to survive these trials.

My father, too, must have suffered a different kind of desperation, one of fear for our safety and fear, somehow, that he wasn't enough, that he wouldn't be able to reunite us.

Sometimes, as women, we forget to consider St. Joseph as a model in our lives. Our feminine disposition might tend to look to Mary as our helper. St. Joseph, however, was Mary's husband—her protector and guide. We see in the story of the Flight to Egypt how Joseph worked in God's plan, and how Mary entrusted herself and her child to her husband. She placed her hope in his courage and fortitude.

Consider the following as you think about the virtue of courage and how you have been cultivating it in your own life:

- Think of a time when you needed more courage and strength than you thought you possessed, like Maria's mom during the time of forced separation from her husband. As you look back, how do you see the virtue of fortitude at work?

- As Mary and Joseph escaped in the night, they could hear the suffering of other families whose children had been killed. What does it mean to have fortitude in the face of someone else's suffering?

- In what areas of your life do you see the greatest need to grow in fortitude?

Reflect on the Meaning: The Flight into Egypt

by Dr. Elizabeth Lev

Becoming a mother tests every woman's strength, but Mary's case was more unnerving than most. Her maternity leave consisted of accepting the meaning of her husband's mysterious dream, urgently preparing for their sudden escape, and forging ahead to resettle in a strange land—learning a foreign language, adapting to new ways, and longing for home.

Their circumstances were not cheerful ones: Joseph had not uprooted the family to seek out a better life in a new land. Rather, the Holy Family was fleeing the powerful King Herod, who was determined to kill their infant son.

The long and expensive trip and the uncertain outcome left the young mother at the mercy of Providence. Leaving behind family and friends to go to the land where their forebears had been enslaved for hundreds of years, Mary could have balked at the whole business and wondered what kind of God would lead her into such a mess. How many times would any other woman be tempted to just stop and say, "Hey, I'm carrying the Son of God here!"

It is in such unfair and unwanted circumstances that the virtue of fortitude shines brightest, and Mary's example is the most compelling of all.

If only I had understood fortitude when I was expecting my first child as a single, unemployed twenty-three-year-old art student in Italy, six thousand miles from home and family. With little faith formation, I looked for female role models. My beloved heroes of Greek mythology were poor examples, always tossed and turned by the swells of fate, usually to an unhappy end—locked in a box, turned into a bear, burned alive; not much guidance there.

The single moms of TV and film were not much better—the most inspirational figures I could find seemed to be Sarah Connor of *Terminator*, Offred of *The Handmaid's Tale*, and Mollie Ubriacco of *Look Who's Talking*. The women around me, my so-called peers, thought that the task of raising a child was too much for me and with the unity of a Greek chorus told me to abort. Only one voice, from across the ocean, urged me to raise this child. That voice was my mother's.

Only later did I learn of the ancient tradition of Mary, *mulier fortis*, celebrated in the Eastern Church as a guardian against heresy and in the medieval West as the hard working and dutiful wife of Proverbs 31. As I studied the art of the Renaissance era, I found that she was not only a warrior against sin but a protectress of those who withstood suffering and setbacks to stay the course. She was Queen of Martyrs, presiding over the men and women who had shown steady witness through the most terrible of trials.

This woman of fortitude didn't demand a world where actions have no consequences, nor did she retreat from and rant against circumstances outside her control. Above all, she certainly did not believe that her own comforts took precedence over the salvation of her soul and the life of her child.

While I had admired the bravery of Antigone defying King Creon or Ripley facing the alien monsters, I saw in Mary fortitude as a more mature virtue, a steadfastness and continuous grace under pressure. Her particular brand of bravery entailed following, not leading, her husband into the desert as she quietly accepted the divine will. Her constant trust in God was so potent that in her seemingly pitiful adventures, she left conversions in her wake—one of the greatest marks of holiness.

When I finally reverted to the Catholic Church, I found an amazing crowd of exceptional women waiting there to greet me—from Mary Magdalene to St. Margaret of Cortona, from St. Catherine of Siena to St. Joan of Arc—women who had persevered through passion, sin, discouragement, betrayal, and death. No matter what dreadful circumstance life might throw my way or that I might bring upon myself, there was always a woman who had borne a similar situation graciously and with grace, before me.

Beyond the clanging of spiritual armor, however, Mary's example of fortitude also bears witness to the quiet graces that are inherent in this virtue. Bravery may seek danger for danger's sake, but fortitude bears the slings and arrows of fortune and soldiers on, overcoming fear and doubt while suffering with serenity.

Artists were quick to depict these intimate moments in beautiful ways. One ancient apocryphal story recounts how Mary and Jesus, looking for shelter in Sotinen, approached an Egyptian temple where there were 375 idols. As soon as they entered, the statues fell to the ground and lay at their feet. The chieftain of the town, a certain Aphrodisius, ran to the temple as soon as he heard and instead of accusing Mary and Jesus, knelt before them and urged his people to do the same. The first fruits of the journey were conversions. A lovely mosaic in St. Mary Major, the oldest basilica to Mary in the West, illustrated this prodigious event for the wealthy Romans of the fifth century.

Artists of the Renaissance depicted another unofficial tale of the flight, of the Holy Family stopping along the route to Egypt, taking respite from the heat and exhaustion. Seated under a fruit tree, Mary expressed a longing to sample a few of its berries. The leaves were out of reach until Jesus ordered it to bend before his mother. Whether seated by a clear stream picking sweet cherries as depicted by Barocci or enjoying an angelic serenade in a sun-drenched glade in Caravaggio's work, these images gently recall that the Lord is not only "my strength and my shield" (Ps 28:7) but also "my strength and my song" (Is 12:2).

Fortitude, albeit always personified as a woman in armor to represent the interior strength this virtue gives, is nonetheless embodied by a woman, symbolic of the softening of the heart to embrace the divine will and remain graceful in steadfast faith.

- Which event in the life of Mary do you think most clearly depicts the virtue of fortitude, and why?

- Who do you think was the most courageous saint, and why? What does the life of this saint teach us about cultivating fortitude in our own lives?

- "This woman of fortitude didn't demand a world where actions have no consequences, nor did she retreat from and rant against circumstances outside her control." Why is the virtue of fortitude especially important in times like these?

Visio Divina: Contemplate the Lord through Sacred Images
by Dr. Elizabeth Lev and Kelly Wahlquist

Federico Barocci, *Rest on the Flight to Egypt,* 1570. Photo ©
Vatican Museums. All rights reserved.

The image for this *visio divina* exercise is *Rest on the Flight to Egypt* by Federico Fiori, also known as Barocci (1570). The original hangs in the Vatican Museums' Pinacoteca (Painting Gallery) in Rome.

Praised by Michelangelo when he was a mere boy, Barocci was considered one of the most talented artists of his time. He developed a technique of blending color to make it appear as if it is changing before our eyes so it seems that we are glimpsing a fleeting moment. His paintings evoke tenderness, charm, and sweetness, often drawing one intimately into the scene.

Find the color image of Barocci's *Rest on the Flight to Egypt* at the front of the book. Spend a few moments gazing on it before you return to the reflection. Use a bookmark to hold your place so you can return to it easily.

Focus your attention on the characters in the painting, noticing their expressions and movements, and the colors, spaces, and shapes that surround them. Ask the Holy Spirit to help you look with the eyes of a prayerful wonderer and contemplate what you see.

A moment in the life of a family is captured, and although this moment appears to be a simple daily event, we know that there is more behind the scene—more in the hearts and minds of these loving parents who are fleeing their home in haste under the threat of death to their son. They are making a strenuous journey with a small child, leaving all that is known and those they love and heading to a foreign country. Yet notice how Barocci depicts tenderness and peace in such a moment. The colors of the morning sun announcing a new day and the elegant detail of each member of the Holy Family—their movements, clothing, and expressions, particularly Jesus' gaze up to his earthly father—all draw us intimately into this simple family meal.

Take in all that is happening: the bubbling water, the light glinting off silver, and the joyful laughter of the child. Notice all that surrounds this serene picture and contemplate the symbolism: the donkey ready to carry this child upon its back; the cherry tree, which often symbolizes heaven; the water needed to sustain life on Mary's right; and the child Jesus grasping the wood handed to him by his father.

Stay in the moment. Are there times in your life when the journey you are on, or the circumstances you face, seem overbearing? Ask Jesus to give you the courage to trust in God's plan for your life. Turn to Mary; ask her to help joy and peace reign in your heart in times of trial and to be with you when you have to do those simple daily tasks and just don't feel like it. Ask her to help you carry them out with joy.

Questions for Group Discussion
by Dr. Carol Younger

Below are questions from various sections of the chapter to help each member of the small group grow in knowledge and faith.
— Kelly Wahlquist

1. Scripture says the Magi came from afar to worship and gave gifts to a baby king unrecognized among his own. You too have traveled far to adore your Savior in your spiritual journey and also in your spiritual experience in this book. It has been costly physically and spiritually to collect gifts to adore him. What do you bring to the manger? Your fidelity in faith: living a good life in the sacraments, teaching your children the faith, and giving

of yourself to others. *These* are the best gifts, the only gift he wants. Share what your heart tells you.

2. Gold, frankincense, and myrrh are presented to the King—then immediately afterward, the slaughter of the innocents in Bethlehem. Satan always brings slaughter, exile, and slavery to the woman and her child. Wherever there are children, women, and family, there follows the hatred of the enemy. Yet God comes to his heirs in our exile, our suffering. What gifts do you bring to help alleviate suffering and pain among your family and friends?

3. In the story, Mary offers the Magi and Adrina hospitality. In ancient times, hospitality included food, shelter, *and safety*. Adrina notices that Mary gives all three of these to the Magi. In her many apparitions, Mary always reminds us to find these gifts of life in the sacraments, especially the Eucharist. She specifically said to Sr. Lucia at Fatima on June 13, 1917: "My Immaculate Heart will be your refuge."[7] Have you been nourished by the sacraments? Has the Church sheltered you? Surely Mary has been your refuge! Share your stories of rescue and safety.

4. Adrina looks at Mary who is unafraid: her trust in God total. Mary has pondered the many events of her journey since the Annunciation, to this moment of flight and exile. Mary's faith is tested and found true. How has your faith been tested and found true? How has God traveled with you in suffering, perhaps even exile? Your faith through times of trouble, threat, even separation from family needs sharing! Courage comes from gazing at how your story and his story come together. Share what you see.

Walking in the New Evangelization
by Kelly Wahlquist

As we conclude this chapter, think about how each aspect has spoken to your heart. What have the scriptures revealed to you? Which qualities of the women in the story resonated with you? How have your eyes been opened to walking in courage? Here are a couple of ways you can continue to reflect upon what you have discovered and grow in virtue.

Virtue in Action

The root of the word courage is *cor*, the Latin word for heart. In its earliest form, the word courage meant to speak one's mind by telling all one's heart. Thomas Merton said, "Just remaining quietly in the presence of God, listening to Him, being attentive to Him requires a lot of courage and know how."[8]

This week, ask the Holy Spirit to help you pursue the greater good, spend ten minutes a day in silent prayer, listen to the sound of his voice—and then share your heart with him.

6.

Gaze with Prudence
(Discovery in the Temple)

A Moment to Ponder
by Kelly Wahlquist

The complexities of family life—even among those who love God and are determined to bring their children up in the faith—are such that parents and pastors alike must continually exercise prudence. In the second epistle to Timothy, St. Paul warned his spiritual son to "avoid disputing about words, which does no good, but only ruins the hearers. Do your best to present yourself to God as one approved, a workman who has no need to be ashamed, rightly handling the word of truth" (2 Tm 2:14–15).

The focus of today's lesson, of Mary and Joseph finding their adolescent son Jesus in the Temple after searching for him for three days, gives us a glimpse of the cardinal virtue of prudence. They did not demand their rights as his parents—and he did not dismiss their authority. Rather, "he went down with them and came to Nazareth, and was obedient to them; and his mother kept all these things in her heart" (Lk 2:51).

As you ponder the scenario from many different angles this week, be sure to take time to ponder how you might cultivate this elusive gift of prudence in your own life, with those within your circle of influence. How might you leave room for the Spirit to work, simply by pondering and praying, rather than demanding and forcing? As a parent, teacher, wife, and daughter, how might you choose to relinquish control to give the Spirit more room to work?

Enter the Scripture
by Sarah Christmyer

Read Luke 2:41–52 before you start.

There comes a moment for every mother when she realizes that the baby she once held in her arms, the child she fed and bathed and taught, is no longer "hers"; in this moment she knows the child is now a man. Maybe it's the day he drives, sets off for college, or gets married. For Mary, surely it was the day Jesus stayed in Jerusalem as the family set out for their home in Nazareth. For twelve years he had obeyed his earthly parents. But sitting in the Temple among the rabbis discussing the Torah, Jesus found himself at home in his heavenly Father's house.

"How is it that you sought me?" he asked his parents. "Did you not know . . ." (Lk 2:49).

No, Mary did not know. But a shift had occurred in Jesus' conscience. He would remain an obedient son, living with his parents until time to move on, but their relationship had changed.

More than any other story from Jesus' early life, the finding of the boy Jesus in the Temple reveals him as both man and God. His identity and purpose are here on display. His father might be Joseph, but his true father is God.

He is the Son. And his purpose? To be about the Father's business, in his Father's house.

Let's take a closer look.

Mary and Joseph go every year to Jerusalem to observe the Passover (see Luke 2:41), as required by the Torah. It's not clear whether Jesus has accompanied them on this annual trek, but even if he has, this time is different. He is twelve years old—nearly a man—and his age will allow him to get closer and see more than he ever has before. This is important. In another year, he will accept the responsibility of the Torah and the requirements of worship as an adult.

Luke picks up "when the feast was ended" (Lk 2:43), but we can imagine what the previous days must have been like for the boy. Perhaps for the first time, he not only ate the Passover meal but also saw the lamb as it was slain and offered. He may have heard the words of the priest and observed the rite in a fresh way, in light of his Torah study. Everything he had learned and that he saw there, *he would one day fulfill.* It's hard to know to what extent Jesus was aware of this, at twelve. But surely the meaning of the Passover filled his mind.

That would certainly account for his actions. The feast ended, his parents and relatives began the walk home, and Jesus stayed behind. How many questions he must have had! It was the practice of the teachers of the Torah on the Sabbath and feast days to sit at the Temple and teach. Perhaps he started out at the edge of the crowd of scholars and rabbis and students. But after three days, by the time his worried parents discovered where he was, he was engrossed in discussion to the point that "all who heard him were amazed at his understanding and his answers" (Lk 2:47).

If they are amazed at the boy's perspicacity, Mary is "astonished" at his treatment of her (Lk 2:48). For three whole days she and Joseph have been searching, and her son apparently hasn't stopped to think that he will be missed or that he belongs with his family. They have been beside themselves with worry. But Jesus is not the one who is lost. He knows exactly where he belongs and who (and whose) he is.

In his answer are his earliest recorded words: "How is it that you sought me? Did you not know that I must be in my Father's house?"

This may be the only glimpse we have of Jesus during the decades between his birth and his public ministry, but it tells us all we need to know about him during this time.

Jesus Knows Who He Is

Mary refers to "his father," Joseph—and Jesus corrects her. "His Father" is also God. This is not to do away with his adoptive earthly father. (Jesus does, after all, return to Nazareth and continue to obey Joseph and Mary, as we read in Luke 2:51.) But Jesus is man *and* God, son of Joseph *and* Son of God. And his heavenly Father takes priority.

Jesus Knows Where He Belongs

He belongs in his heavenly Father's house. The Temple was the place of God's presence, the place where he was worshiped, the place where his work was done. All of this would change one day, but it is in the Temple that Jesus (the living Temple!) is most clearly at home.

Jesus Knows His Purpose

"In my Father's house" also means "about my father's business." Jesus' purpose is to obey God and carry out the mission for which he came. He would grow in wisdom over time (see Luke 2:52), which may mean he had things to learn yet about that mission. But his use of "must" shows that doing God's business is imperative for him. As an adult, he'll use the same word on several occasions to show he's under a divine mandate to preach and do the works of God and suffer and die and be raised.[1] The obedient will of the adult Son can be seen in the boy in the Temple.

All this might be clear in retrospect, but it did not make sense to Mary and Joseph. They, too, are "growing up," as all parents do as their children grow and challenge them in various ways. This experience must have been very painful. Mary "kept all these things in her heart" (Lk 2:51), and they evidently remained so vivid in her mind that she told them to Luke. By then, maybe she had made the connection: that three days of panicked searching for a son who had disappeared ended in discovery and a new and deeper appreciation of his person and mission.

Twenty years later, another three days of darkness and longing ended in discovery as well. Did she remember her own cry of "Son, why have you treated us so?" (Lk 2:48) when she heard her son cry out from the Cross, "My God, my God, why hast thou forsaken me?" (Mt 27:46). Did she realize he was, even and especially then, about his Father's business?

The "sword" prophesied by Simeon had begun to pierce her heart, but it did not kill her. Pain opened out onto something greater. As St. John Paul II said about this incident, "Jesus brings [Joseph and Mary] into the mystery of that suffering which leads to joy." He then draws attention to the change in their relationship: "At the temple in Jerusalem, in this prelude to his saving mission, Jesus associates his Mother with himself; no longer is she merely the One who gave him birth, but the Woman who, through her own obedience to the Father's plan, can co-operate in the mystery of Redemption."[2]

Prayer

Lord, open my eyes; help me find Jesus! When he is hidden, let me learn from Mary to ponder and seek and eventually find the One I seek. Thank you that he is about the Father's business—even in the temple of my heart.

Gaze Upon Jesus: Mary, Mother of God
A story by Stephanie Landsem

"Ima, are you coming with us to Jerusalem?" Jesus asked me, dumping an armload of wood next to the cooking fire.

I smiled up at him. He spent most of his time working with Joseph, but he still made sure I had plenty of wood for the fire. "Of course," I answered. By Passover of next year, he would be thirteen years old and a son of the Law. "This year is special, your last as a child. I wouldn't miss it."

"Abba will be glad," he said as he snuck a round of bread from the fire. I swatted at him with my wooden spoon and missed. He ran off, laughing and tossing the hot bread between his hands. Sometimes he still acted like a child, and that made me smile.

Our group was large, at least twenty relations from Nazareth alone, and when we went through Cana, we were joined by even more. It was a joyful group, praising the Lord and sharing news of our families. Jesus walked with the boys his age and only found us when he was hungry. By the time we reached Bethany, Joseph's strength was waning, and we were glad to rest at the home of our kinsman, Sirach, and his daughters, Martha and Mary.

"It may be Joseph's last Passover," Martha said, her eyes filled with concern as she prepared unleavened bread for the many friends and relatives staying with them.

"Martha, how can you say that?" Mary, her younger sister, scolded. "Joseph has many years left with his family."

But Martha was right, I knew with a sadness in my heart. Joseph had grown frail over the winter and a persistent cough left him weak and breathless.

Martha slid the rounds of dough into a clay oven. "You are fortunate Jesus can take on more of his father's work, now that he is almost a man. He will take care of you."

I pondered Martha's words. More than a dozen years had passed since the angel had come to me, since the birth of my child in a cave in Bethlehem. And then, the prophecy of the old man, Simeon, in the Temple. Joseph had been a good father to Jesus, taking us to safety in Egypt when Herod Agrippa threatened, bringing us back to Nazareth after Herod's death. Everyone in Nazareth believed Joseph to be Jesus' father, but I had never forgotten the angel's words to me. I knew in my heart that my son's work would not be with stone and wood.

But what would his Father's work be? That, I did not know.

After the sacrifices were made in the Temple and the Passover meal eaten, we took our leave of Martha and Mary and their father, thanking them for their hospitality. The journey home would be long, but our caravan was large and our spirits filled with Passover joy. The first day we traveled far, singing the songs of our people and talking of all we had seen and heard in Jerusalem. When the sun sank low and the cool wind came from the west, we found a meadow in which to make camp, set up sentries, and passed dried fish, almonds, and figs to the children.

"Where is Jesus?" I poured a cup of watered wine for Joseph, who had settled before the fire. His face was drawn and his cough had worsened.

"I thought he was with Zevulan and his boys," Joseph shook his head. "But they haven't seen him all day."

I felt a flutter of concern, but pushed it aside. He could be with any of the families. "Perhaps Jotham and Ruth?" I left Joseph and weaved through the camp. Ruth had not seen my son. "Is Jesus with you?" I asked each family. By the time I returned to Joseph, the night was dark and my heart was pounding. No one had seen Jesus since Jerusalem.

I did not sleep that night. *Lord my God, your love reaches to heaven; your faithfulness to the clouds.* I asked for the Lord's faithfulness now. *Be with us now, oh Lord, remain with your servants in our hour of need.*

The first lightening of the eastern sky found Joseph and I leading our donkey back toward Jerusalem. Joseph moved faster than he had in years, his breath wheezing in his chest. I hurried beside him. Even the donkey seemed to sense our urgency and had no interest in the grass beside the road.

Do not be afraid. The angel's words whispered to me with every scuffing step. *The Lord is with you.*

When we reached Bethany, Sirach opened the gates of his home in surprise. "He's not here," he said to my question, shaking his head. "It is coming on dark. Rest here tonight. We will search for him as soon as the sun rises."

I did not sleep for a second night but waited for the morning sun. Praying to the Lord, wondering what had become of my son. *Do not be afraid.*

We entered the gates of Jerusalem as the seven silver trumpets called out from the Temple walls. "I'll ask at each gate," Sirach told us. Joseph and I went to everyone we knew. Zebediah in the upper city hadn't seen our son but joined the search. His brother, a seller of grain, promised to watch for him in the marketplace.

"Perhaps he is with Miriam and her boys," Joseph said.

Miriam opened her gate to us, the surprise on her face shattering my hope. She ushered us inside where her sons, Joses and James, were playing with sticks. She was heavy with child and had told me secretly when we had seen her at the Passover feast that she was sure this was a girl. "Oh, Mary." She took my hand in hers when I told her of our search. "I pray you find him. I will send word to everyone I know."

We left Miriam and retraced our steps during the feast. If Elizabeth were here, what would she do? *Trust in the Lord,* I could hear her say to me. *Wait on his faithfulness.*

I did trust in the Lord. And yet my son was missing . . . I could not rest until I found him.

The scent of burnt sacrifice and incense hung in the streets near the Temple. Joseph asked at every corner, but no one had seen a lone Galilean boy. We rested in the shade of the Temple, where the beggars and cripples lined up to beg for alms. "Remember how we found no place to stay in Bethlehem?" Joseph asked me.

I remembered. The streets of Bethlehem had been just as crowded. Joseph had asked at every inn and house while I knew my time approached.

"The Lord was faithful to us," he said, taking my hand.

Yes, the Lord was faithful. He had sent us help in the most unlikely form: a young woman, crippled and child-like, to give what little shelter she had. I knew that, yet when I thought of Jesus in these crowded streets—alone and perhaps lost and hungry—I couldn't help the worry that weakened my legs. I looked up to the Temple mount, where Simeon had made his prophecy. It seemed like just yesterday. He had said a sword would pierce my heart. Indeed, separation from my son was a sword in my heart. Was this the moment he had spoken of?

I remembered another night in Bethlehem—a terrible, tragic night. When Joseph—strong and determined—had led us through the dark streets and out of Herod's deadly grip. My husband had heeded the angel's warning that saved Jesus from Herod's wrath. He had protected us, sustained us, cherished us these twelve years. Joseph's constancy had been a blessing from the Lord. Surely, his faithfulness had not been in vain?

I trust in you, oh Lord. But I would continue to search for Jesus.

As the sun moved into the west, we searched the lower market. "Stay close to me," Joseph said as he hobbled along the narrow street lined with grimy shops and smelling of tanners' hides and rotting fruit. My eyes burned from the dust, and my head ached from sleepless nights. Women with baskets on their heads and ragged clothes on their backs turned to stare at us. Men stopped arguing and narrowed their eyes as we passed. Joseph asked a wine seller with black teeth if he'd seen a boy alone, perhaps lost and looking for his father. The man spat a brown puddle into the dust and shook his head. "Run off, did he?"

I refused that idea as we left the lower city. Jesus wouldn't run off. Yes, he teased and laughed like other boys. He was clumsy and sometimes broke things and often stumbled over his own feet. But he never disobeyed. He loved Joseph and he loved me. He would never do something that would hurt us. So, where was he?

As we passed steps leading to the pool of Siloam, Joseph stumbled. I took his arm, leading us to the wall where he leaned, pale and panting, against the cool stone. Was Martha right that Joseph would not see another Passover feast in Jerusalem? How could I do without the man who had believed in the angel's words when all that he knew told him otherwise? The man who had raised Jesus as his own yet knew the child was from God? As if sensing my troubled heart, Joseph took my hands in his and bowed his head toward mine. "Lord of heaven and earth, your steadfast love is always before our eyes, let us walk in your faithfulness."

I felt the Lord's peace fill me as it had so many times before. The Lord's love was truly always before our eyes, if we would but see it. In the generations of Israel, had the Lord not allowed evil and made good come from it? Daniel in the den of lions, Joseph sold into slavery in Egypt. The

Lord had saved his people time and again, proving his love and faithfulness.

Would he not do the same for his own son?

We turned back toward the upper city, Joseph leaning on me as we climbed the steep stairs. "Mary!" I heard the call behind me. "Mary, Joseph, wait!"

I turned to find Zilpah, Miriam's mother, laboring to catch up with us. She bent forward, catching her breath before she could speak. "The Temple," she panted. "Jesus is in the Temple."

Relief weakened my legs. I clutched Joseph's arm. The Temple? He was not yet a son of the law. He had no sacrifice to offer. Why was he there?

Zilpah followed, her heavy breath sounding behind me, as we hurried up the stepped street and over the bridge that led to the Temple. The Huldah Gates brought us to the dim underground corridors of the Temple mount. Joseph seemed to forget his weariness as we rushed up the stone steps to the Court of the Gentiles.

"There," Zilpah pointed, blinking in the rays of the setting sun, "on the steps to the Beautiful Gate."

There he was. Jesus. My boy.

The court stretched for an eternity. I stumbled forward, unable to get to my son fast enough. I bounded up the fifteen steps that led to the golden doors of the Beautiful Gate. He was here. He was safe. *Thank you, my Lord and my God, thank you,* was the only prayer my pounding heart could form.

Finally, I stood in front of Jesus. He wore a clean robe and his dark hair was combed. Relief rushed through me, weakening my legs. He looked . . . fine. I clasped my hands in front of me, wishing I could throw my arms around him. "My son," I breathed, "why have you treated us so?"

I'm not sure what I was expecting . . . sorrow, perhaps. An apology for worrying us. But Jesus instead looked at me, confused, as if I had spoken another language.

Only then did I look around, and what I saw only added to my astonishment. Jesus—my son of only twelve years—sat in a place of honor on the top of the fifteenth step. Around him were men of all ages—scribes with their pointed blue hats, Pharisees with wide phylacteries and long beards, Sadducees in fine robes.

"Is this your son?" One of the Pharisees approached Joseph, who had come to stand behind me. "He has been here for days, and his wisdom has astounded us all."

A white-haired rabbi exclaimed from his place at Jesus feet. "His understanding of the law . . . his knowledge of the prophets. It is beyond all we've ever heard."

"He is just a boy," the long-nosed priest marveled. "And from Galilee."

The old rabbi turned on the priest. "Whoever he is, he comes from God."

Joseph stepped forward and spoke in a low voice. "Jesus, we have been looking for you for three days."

Jesus rose to his feet, his face brightened by the beams of sunlight glinting off the Beautiful Gate. For a moment, it was as if I didn't recognize my own child. "Why were you looking for me?" He sounded truly perplexed. "Did you not know that I must be in my Father's house?"

The priest snorted incredulously. "His father's house?" He turned to Joseph. "Are you not his father? If he is your son, tell us!"

Joseph did not answer.

For twelve years—through the bright days of his childhood and the dark hours of the night—I had pondered. I had wondered what it all meant.

The message of an angel, *Do not be afraid.*

The cry of Elizabeth, *Blessed be the fruit of your womb.*

The prophecy in the Temple, *A sword will pierce your heart.*

The homage of Magi, *Where is the newborn king?*

And finally, this desperate search for Jesus. *Did you not know?*

Perhaps I was beginning to know the Lord's purpose. Jesus would leave me to do his Father's work. The sword in my heart—the one Simeon had promised—was yet to come. But in his faithfulness, the Lord had not forgotten his handmaiden. In his goodness, the Lord was making me ready for that day. Ready for that sword. Ready to give up my son to the will of his Father.

I am the handmaid of the Lord. Let it be to me according to your Word.

I stood beside my husband and took his hand in mine. The priest waited, his question unanswered. No, Jesus was not Joseph's son. Jesus was the Messiah . . . heralded by an angel, known in the womb, born in a cave. Jesus was a king proclaimed by prophets and worshiped by pagans.

But not yet. His time had not yet come. I knew that deep in my mother's heart.

I held out my other hand. "Come, my son." For now, he would remain with Joseph and me, growing in wisdom and grace, and when his Father called him to do his work, I would be ready.

Jesus took my hand. Together, the three of us started the journey home.

The Lord, my God, is faithful. Yes, the Lord was with me. I held tight to my son's hand, while I still could. *He is with me, even now.*

In Search of Prudence: Discovery in the Temple

by Maria Morera Johnson

The wisest man who ever lived, King Solomon, recounts in the book of Wisdom how he came to receive such remarkable spiritual gifts.

> *Therefore I prayed, and understanding was given me;*
> *I called upon God, and the spirit of wisdom came to me.*
> *I preferred her to scepters and thrones,*
> *and I accounted wealth as nothing in comparison with her. . . .*
> *For it is an unfailing treasure for men;*
> *those who get it obtain friendship with God,*
> *commended for the gifts that come from instruction.*
> *(Ws 7:7–8, 14)*

In this passage we see the secrets of obtaining a heart of discernment and prudence: prayer, sacrifice, and an unquenchable thirst to know and obey God. If we are willing to put his will above our own comfort, above our own desires, above every other thing, as we find in the testimony that follows . . . the gift of prudence is a flower that bears abundant fruit. —Kelly Wahlquist

As an educator, I always straddled the fence between justice and mercy. On the one hand, students earned grades based on their performance. On the other hand, perhaps their performance was affected by circumstances outside their control. Did the internet go down when they were in the middle of a test? Did they have a sleepless night because of staying up with a sick child? Did they misread a set of directions? Or did they go out to a club instead of study for an exam?

I couldn't know the truth, but I could listen with an open mind and make a decision based on my conscience. If I felt I had enough facts, I could make a decision that would promote the good of the student. Sometimes, the good of the student meant a lesson in consequences and my denial to revisit a poor grade. Other times, mercy led me to offer a second chance. I almost always opted to lead with mercy, even in those cases when I felt I might not have all the facts.

At the end of the day, I made decisions that would bring me peace. I practiced the virtue of prudence in my decision-making, and when I could, helped the students also exercise prudence by examining their actions and decisions, and draw their own conclusions on the matter.

When I wavered and feared I was making the wrong decision, I called to mind Jesus, who was also a teacher. How did he handle his detractors? The disobedient? The contrary folks with hidden agendas? It made me look at each circumstance in relation to the student and not necessarily a broad application of the rule. I allowed mercy to temper judgment. Put another way, I could deliver the right judgment with mercy.

The *Catechism of the Catholic Church* explains this process of discernment:

> Prudence is the virtue that disposes practical reason to discern our true good in every circumstance and to choose the right means of achieving it; "the prudent man looks where he is going" [Prv 14:15]. "Keep sane and sober for your prayers" [1 Pt 4:7]. Prudence is "right reason in action," writes St. Thomas Aquinas, following Aristotle [St. Thomas Aquinas, STh II-II, 47, 2]. It is not to be confused with timidity or fear, nor with duplicity or dissimulation. It is called *auriga virtutum* (the charioteer of the virtues); it guides the other virtues by setting rule and measure. It is prudence that immediately guides the judgment of conscience. The prudent man determines and directs his conduct in accordance with this judgment. With the help of this virtue we apply moral principles to particular cases without error and overcome doubts about the good to achieve and the evil to avoid. (*CCC*, 1806)

Prudence helps guide our actions so that we do the right thing in our circumstances. Sometimes doing the right thing is not necessarily the expected thing. That can lead to confusion, and even, in some cases, the questioning of our motives.

Yet there's nothing like the calm conviction we can have when we know we have arrived at the right conclusion, even if we face opposition. In popular culture, we might call that standing by our principles.

Consider the following as you think about the virtue of prudence and how you have been cultivating it in your own life:

- When was the last time you asked God for wisdom when you were in a situation that had no clear resolution? What was the way of prudence?

- St. Thomas Aquinas said that prudence is "right reason in action." Does this mean that the prudent choice will always be spontaneously self-evident? What is the difference between prudence and impulsivity?

- Given the definition of prudence from the *Catechism*, what are some ways that we can practice prudence—and teach it to our children?

Reflect on the Meaning: Discovery of Jesus in the Temple
by Joan Lewis

One sunny day when I was three and a half years old, I wanted to visit my paternal grandmother, who was very ill in the hospital. I had been to the hospital one other time with my parents who, knowing how Ganny loved flowers, had brought a big bouquet to her room. I too wanted to bring her a gift to make her happy, so I put several magazines into a big paper bag and started out on my journey. Alone. Without telling Mom and Dad. Imprudent but, after all, what does a three-year-old know of prudence?

I thought I knew the route that Dad had driven, so I just started walking. I walked down our street, past the neighbors' homes, made some turns, crossed some train tracks, saw some stores and buildings I thought I knew, and kept on walking. After a while, a squad car stopped and a policeman came over and asked if my name was, by any chance, Joan. I smiled and said, "Yes, how do you know?"

The familiar, biblical refrain: My dad to my mom, "Is Joannie with you?" My mom to my dad, "No, I thought she was with you in your workshop!" And that's how they discovered I was missing and, after a thorough search of the house and garden, called the police.

Mom told me this story when I was well into adulthood, and to be honest, I've often thought of what that moment must have meant for my mom and dad—their beloved firstborn was missing!—when I read the gospel story of Jesus in the Temple or reflected on the fifth Joyful Mystery, the Finding of the Child Jesus in the Temple.

I saw the anguish and fear on my parents faces turn to joy when I was found by the policeman. There were tears of joy and breathtaking (literally) hugs and *so* much love! And understanding: they loved why I decided to take a walk but also admonished me not to do so again without first telling them.

Is that what Mary and Joseph felt as well? How did they act? What do we learn from St. Luke's account? (See Luke 2:41–52.)

There's so much we don't know about this story. Did Mary and Joseph journey home together or, as was the custom in a big caravan, was Mary with the women and Joseph with the men, thus presumably also with Jesus? Had they told Jesus to stay with them in Jerusalem, not to go off on his own? Had they set up a meeting place and time for their journey home?

We don't have the answers to those practical questions, but we can reflect on what we learned about virtues in this story. Two jump out rather easily—humility and obedience—but a third is also a standout—the cardinal virtue of prudence.

The *Catechism of the Catholic Church* defines prudence as "the virtue that disposes practical reason to discern our true good in every circumstance and to choose the right means of achieving it" (*CCC*, 1806). Prudence has also been defined as "the intellectual virtue that rightly directs particular human acts toward a good end."[3]

I personally love St. Thomas Aquinas's definition as it is short, sweet, and to the point: prudence is "right reason in action." In this story, prudence is clearly linked to Mary, the Mother. In twenty words, expressing her puzzlement and anxiety, Mary asked her son why he had remained behind in Jerusalem.

Jesus' answer was puzzling: "Did you not know that I must be in my Father's house?" (Lk 2:49).

Mary, not understanding her son's answer, reacted prudently: " And his mother kept all these things in her heart" (Lk 2:51). Her prudence consists in not reacting rashly to her son's words, words that might even have been hurtful. Instead Mary "ponders" these things in her heart, she discerns, and she thinks things through, thus, as St. Thomas said, "right reason in action." Just as she did at the Annunciation, the Visitation, and the Nativity, once again in Jerusalem, Mary acted prudently, with right reason.

As Fr. Alexis Lepicier, O.S.M., wrote on his blog, *Little Office of the Blessed Virgin Mary*, "It was prudence which restrained the glorious Virgin from ever proceeding with precipitancy; it was this same virtue which prompted her . . . to weigh with a wise deliberation the motives of her every action, to decide with calmness the course to be pursued, and to follow in all her actions the light of reason and faith."[4]

As I read, researched, reflected, and prayed about this mystery of the Rosary and the virtue of prudence, I realized I could not remember the last time I had heard anyone use that word—prudence. Do we even have time to be prudent, to ponder, to think things out in order to put "right reason into action"? Do we make time to be prudent? We live in a fast-paced world that wants decisions and answers to be made, not now, not today, but yesterday. But that's rashness, the opposite of prudence. Are we instead prudent? Do we ponder, discern, take the time to think things through? Do we try to avoid rashness and all its negative consequences?

If not, the answer is to slow down, to make the time to imitate Mary, especially in prudence, as this will surely guide us in the practice of all the other virtues. Let's ask ourselves in any situation that requires a course of action: What would Mary do?

And maybe, if we live our lives prudently, we will be a little like Jesus: "And Jesus advanced [in] wisdom and age and favor before God and man" (Lk 2:52, NABRE).

- So often we face situations that would have been unthinkable to Mary: making a cross-country phone call, choosing a television program, or popping lunch into the microwave. What does it mean, then, to cultivate prudence by asking ourselves, "What would Mary do?"

- When Jesus replied to his parents that he had to be in his Father's house, his parents must have been perplexed! What does prudence do when we are faced with puzzling or even seemingly contradictory events, to take steps to "put right reason into action"?

Visio Divina: Contemplate the Lord through Sacred Images
by Dr. Elizabeth Lev and Kelly Wahlquist

Angelo Biancini, *Jesus in the Temple*, 1958. Photo © Vatican Museums. All rights reserved.

The image for this *visio divina* exercise is called *Jesus in the Temple* by Angelo Biancini (1958). The original hangs in the Vatican Museums' Gallery of Contemporary Art in Rome.

Angelo Biancini studied art in Florence, Italy, during the 1930s—a turbulent decade that saw the growing power of Benito Mussolini and the beginning of the Second World War—and remarkably, kept his faith. Sculpting in bronze, clay, and marble during an age when form, truth, and order were either cast aside by the avant garde or harnessed for the propaganda purposes of tyrannical regimes, Biancini produced elusive figures, forcing the viewer to pay close attention in order to see them emerge from the surface of the clay.

Find the color image of Biancini's *Jesus in the Temple* at the front of the book. Spend a few moments gazing on it before you return to the reflection. Use a bookmark to hold your place so you can return to it easily.

Focus your heart on the characters in the painting, noticing their expressions and movements, and the colors, spaces, and shapes that surround them. Ask the Holy Spirit to help you look with the eyes of a prayerful wonderer and contemplate what you see.

A child is lost. Frantic parents retrace their steps, asking, "Has anyone has seen the boy?" Their hearts cry out, imploring the assistance of the Lord. The gnarled clay makes present the confusion of the search, while the sharp, angular strokes evoke the lacerating fears of the parents—is he hurt, frightened, alone?

Though the texture and configuration of the art may elicit the emotions felt by the parents, the objects and the characters in the piece tell a different story. The columns frame two tall, erect heads at the entrance to the temple. The search is over; Jesus is found. The foreground figures, rounded and curved, lean toward the Christ Child as if already attracted by truth.

Put yourself in this scene, not as the frantic parent but as one in the Temple. Jesus is sitting among the teachers, listening to them, asking them questions, and answering their questions with great understanding and wisdom. What is this amazing child doing? He is drawing souls to him. What do you feel as you sit before this child? Picture the moment his parents first see him. What expression do you see on his mother's face? What do you feel in your heart for her? Do you hear her speak to the child?

Scripture tells us that although Mary may have found her son's response puzzling ("Did you not know that I must be in my Father's house?"), she did not continue to ask questions. Rather, she kept all that had transpired in her heart. How do you respond to God's mysterious ways in your life? Is there an area of your life now where you are suffering and struggle to understand why God would allow such suffering?

Turn to your mother, Mary. Let her gaze comfort you. Ask her to help you ponder in your heart the will of God when you encounter surprising and sometimes painful mysteries in your life and to help you respond with prudence.

Questions for Group Discussion
by Dr. Carol Younger

Below are questions from various sections of the chapter to help each member of the small group grow in knowledge and faith.
—Kelly Wahlquist

1. We gaze at Jesus, who knows who he is, where he belongs, and what his mission is. Reflect: Who are you, to whom do you belong, and what is your mission?

Look back at when you (a) realized you think differently than your parents, value different things, and (b)
left your birth family for college, for marriage, or to live
somewhere else. You now have a separate mission, a
separate life goal. Gazing at these scenes, does Jesus
look at you and speak to your heart? What does he say?
Share what you see and hear.

2. After being found, Jesus returns to Mary and Joseph's
   home. The Holy Family reflected the Holy Trinity in
   their home. Mary and Joseph grew in wisdom and grace,
   just as Jesus did in obedience to his divine Father. How
   are you obedient and faithful to the Father of Jesus, our
   Father? How do you build virtue in your relationships
   with family and friends, and in yourself? Share those
   secrets of virtue-building.

3. "Jesus is in the Temple," Zilpah tells Mary. And Mary
   rushes there with Joseph! Is it any wonder that Mary
   rushes to us in countless apparitions over many centuries? She comes looking for us, wanting us to return
   with her to the Holy Family dwelling. She wants us to
   be temples of the Holy Spirit through the sacraments
   of the Church. Gaze on Mary's Immaculate Heart, her
   pure devotion to Jesus, her protective motherhood of
   the Savior, her child. Ask her to mother you, to protect
   you, to come looking for you when you are lost. What
   is your most urgent request of her today?

4. Just as he did in the Jerusalem Temple, Jesus comes and
   sits within us, looks at us, asks us questions, gives us
   answers, and goes about the business of his Father within our souls. What has he said to you recently? What has
   he asked? Have you asked him to stay with you while
   you grow in grace and wisdom? One day, in eternity,

you will see him gaze at your virtue and love of him. How do you want to be able to respond to his look of love?

Walking in the New Evangelization
by Kelly Wahlquist

As we conclude this chapter, think about how each aspect has spoken to your heart. What have the scriptures revealed to you? Which qualities of the women in the story resonated with you? How have your eyes been opened to walking in prudence? Here are a couple of ways you can continue to reflect upon what you have discovered and grow in virtue.

Virtue in Action

St. Francis of Assisi said, "Blessed is the one . . . who is not anxious to speak, but who reflects prudently on what he is to say and the manner in which he is to reply."[5] Often our emotions encourage us to do one thing, and right reason prompts us to act in a different way. The next decision you have to make, do not be anxious to speak but rather follow the three aspects of prudence: counsel, judgment, and decisiveness. Pray for the grace of prudence before taking action. Then, gather the information needed to make a good decision. Ask the Holy Spirit to guide you to discern the best course of action. And then just do it; be decisive.

Since prudence directs all virtues so that we choose the true good for ourselves in every life circumstance, we need to turn to God daily and ask humbly for holy prudence. As you fall asleep each night, pray: *Lord, give me prudence, so that I may live the virtues through your grace during this life, and enter into your loving gaze in eternity.*

Conclusion

by Kelly Wahlquist

Have you ever said something totally obvious and then chuckled at the fact that you said it out loud? I have a friend who, whenever I say something as crazy as, "This water is wet," quickly chimes in with, "Your ability to perceive the obvious would amaze the most casual observer." Though it makes me laugh, I know I am not alone in making self-evident statements.

Once, when my daughter Annika did the same thing, I cleverly said, "Nice point, Captain Obvious," to which she quickly retorted, "Thank you, General Sarcasm." Now, while both are examples of our ability to recognize the apparent, in actuality, women do more than just notice the basics. Women perceive details that surpass mere sight. Women look beyond the obvious and see the person—the whole person—and the entire situation, as Dr. Deborah Savage reminds us: "In *Mulieris Dignitatum*, John Paul argues that the feminine genius is grounded in the fact that all women have the capacity to be mothers—and that this capacity, whether fulfilled in a physical or spiritual sense, orients her toward the other, toward persons."[1]

Oriented toward the other, women see with the eyes of the heart. We don't just see people and objects; we detect how they each relate to one another. All the circumstances—physical, emotional, and spiritual—that make up a situation come into focus, and with them comes a natural concern and a desire to tend to the cares of the person in need. Women inherently focus on the dignity of the person, yet at the same time take in all the details in the periphery, noting the effect each has on the other. This beautiful combination of sensitivity and intuition is what propels women from merely seeing to gazing—looking upon another with love.

This is how the biblical and fictional women in the stories you have read in this book have looked upon Jesus. They have each fixed their loving gaze upon him as he grew in wisdom and stature. Each woman saw past what appeared obvious to the world and recognized the plan of God; she saw beyond the natural and embraced the supernatural. Where the world saw a young pregnant woman, Elizabeth saw the mother of her Lord. As little Lila looked into the peaceful face of a newborn babe, she gazed upon Love Incarnate and experienced the peace that surpasses all understanding. The people of Jerusalem watched a poor couple offer two turtledoves for sacrifice at the Temple, but Anna gazed with reverence upon God's great offering— the salvation of the world. To onlookers, they were merely a young family driven into exile and forced to leave the comfort and familiarity of their homeland, but with the stroke of the brush, Barocci created a scene that expressed the serenity and joy that come when we have the courage to surrender to God's plan for our lives.

Every moment, from the Annunciation to finding the twelve-year-old Jesus in the Temple, from the beginning of Jesus' public ministry at the wedding of Cana to the foot of the Cross, Mary surrendered her will and lived in accordance with God's will. She lived the virtues. Mary is the example of perfect humility, patience, charity, reverence, courage, and prudence. Mary demonstrates how living virtuous, holy lives opens the eyes of our hearts, allows us to see beyond the visible, and enables us to trust God and all he has planned for us. Mary teaches us that it is faith that allows us to see God present in all those situations where we think he is absent. She teaches us that God has fixed his gaze on us and he will never take his loving eyes off of us.

There is a transforming power in the gaze of one who loves you. Jesus has fixed his gaze on you. "This is not just any man who looks at another; it is 'the Lord,' whose eyes peer into the depths of the heart, into the deepest secrets of a person's soul," Pope Benedict XVI tells us.[2]

Pope Francis adds to this, "The gaze of Jesus always makes us worthy, gives us dignity. It is a look that always lifts us up, and never leaves you in your place, never lets us down, never humiliates. It invites you to get up—a look that brings you to grow, to move forward, that encourages you."[3]

At the beginning of this book, Teresa said, "No one walks away from viewing the *Pietà* or the Sistine Chapel unaffected." It is my hope and prayer, my dear sister, that as you go forth from this book, you do so with a transformed heart. As you enter into the advents, surprises, joys, and difficulties of your life, may you be encouraged by the women who gazed upon Jesus in the scriptures, in their stories, and in their personal reflections. May you ask the Lord to help you contemplate the graces of God that surround you with the eyes of a prayerful wonderer. And may you go forth in your mission as a woman in the New Evangelization, gazing anew upon Jesus and allowing his gaze to lift you up until one day you meet him, face to face, and bask in all his glory.

Your face, oh Lord, is what my heart seeks.

Notes

Foreword

1. Teresa of Avila, *Autobiography of St. Teresa of Avila*, trans. E. Allison Peers (Mineola, NY: Dover, 2010), loc. 2198 of 7227, Kindle.

2. Sarah Young, *Jesus Always: Embracing Joy in His Presence* (Nashville, TN: Thomas Nelson, 2016), 212.

Introduction

1. Mark Haydu, *Meditations on Vatican Art* (Liguori, MO: Liguori, 2013), ix.

2. The *Gaze Upon Jesus* accompanying journal is available at www. CatholicVineyard.com. Those participating in a WINE book club, as well as those reading the book on their own, will benefit from the additional guided reflection found in this journal. Ample space is provided to record your own thoughts and reflection as you move through the book.

1. Gaze with Humility (The Annunciation)

1. Joseph Ratzinger, *Jesus of Nazareth: The Infancy Narratives*, trans. Philip J. Whitmore (New York: Image, 2012), 27–28.

2. Ratzinger, *Jesus of Nazareth*, 29.

3. Joseph Ratzinger, "Hail, Full of Grace: Elements of Marian Piety according to the Bible," in Hans Urs von Balthasar and Joseph Cardinal Ratzinger, *Mary: The Church at the Source*, trans. Adrian Walker (San Francisco: Ignatius Press, 2005), 70.

4. John Paul II, *Laborem Exercens* (September 14, 1981), 6.

5. Brooke Williams Deely, ed., *Pope John Paul II Speaks on Women* (Washington, DC: Catholic University of America Press, 2014), 127.

6. John Paul II, *Mulieris Dignitatem* (August 15, 1988), 5.

7. Benedict Ashley, *Justice in the Church: Gender and Participation* (Washington, DC: Catholic University of America Press, 1996), 137.

8. Mary is said to have *pondered* here; she *thought*. Though she is often described as reflecting on all these things "in her heart," the English translation of the Hebrew word for "heart" (*leb*) misses the mark. It is a reference, not to feeling, but to the seat of the person. In Hebrew, *leb* includes the inner man, the mind, will, and heart, that is, the whole of the person, including the intellect. For an account of the epistemology at work here, see Pia Francesca de Solenni, *A Hermeneutic of Aquinas's Mens through a Sexually Differentiated Epistemology: Towards an Understanding of Woman as Imago Dei* (Rome: Edizioni Universita della Santa Croze, 2003).

173

9. Pius XII, "Papal Directives for the Woman of Today: Allocution to the Congress of the International Union of Catholic Women's Leagues in Rome, Italy" (September 11, 1947).

10. Stephen J. Binz, *Transformed by God's Word: Discovering the Power of Lectio and Visio Divina* (Notre Dame, IN: Ave Maria, 2016), 10.

2. Gaze with Patience (The Visitation)

1. See Genesis 25:21–23 (Jacob); Judges 13:2–5 (Samson); and 1 Samuel 1 (Samuel).

2. See, for example, 1 Chronicles 15:28, 16:4; and 2 Chronicles 5:13.

3. See *Catechism*, 489. Chief among these songs is the Song of Hannah in 1 Samuel 2.

3. Gaze with Charity (The Nativity)

1. Gerard Manley Hopkins, S.J., trans., "Adoro te devote," http://www.rosarychurch.net/mystic/aquinas.html.

2. Some Catholic Bible scholars reject the idea that this census was truly "universal," but it is intended to underscore the significance of the event of Christ's birth to both the Jewish and Roman worlds. (See *The Catholic Study Bible: Third Edition* [New York: Oxford University Press, 2013], 1438.)

3. The Priene Inscription: *Orientis Graeci Inscriptiones Selectae* (OGIS), 458. For an English translation, see http://pages.uoregon.edu/klio/tx/re/asia-dec.htm.

4. As Jesus will tell his disciples, "Peace I leave with you; my peace I give to you; not as the world gives do I give to you. Let not your hearts be troubled, neither let them be afraid" (John 14:27).

5. Thérèse of Lisieux, *Autobiography of a Saint*, trans. Ronald Knox (London: Harvill, 1958), 235.

6. Teresa of Calcutta, *Love: A Fruit Always in Season*, ed. Dorothy S. Hunt (San Francisco, CA: Ignatius Press, 1987), 129.

4. Gaze with Reverence (The Presentation)

1. The Protoevangelium of James, *New Advent*, paragraphs 7–8, accessed May 14, 2018, http://www.newadvent.org/fathers/0847.htm.

2. Benedict XVI, Homily on the Feast of the Presentation of the Lord (February 2, 2011).

3. "Firstborn" does not indicate the first among multiple children but the first child to "open the womb," whether or not others follow.

4. Miriam led Israel in song after God's triumph over Egypt at the Red Sea (see Exodus 15:20–21); Deborah sang God's praise after Israel's victory over Sisera in Judges 5.

5. Randall Smith, "Reverence and Respect," *The Catholic Thing*, November 19, 2015, https://www.thecatholicthing.org/2015/11/19/reverence-and-respect.

6. Romano Guardini, *Learning the Virtues That Lead You to God* (Bedford, NH: Sophia Institute Press, 2013), 59.

5. Gaze with Courage (The Flight to Egypt)

1. On page 1256, the *Catholic Study Bible* notes tell us, "Hosea dates the real beginning of Israel from the time of the exodus. Matthew 2:15 applies this text to the return of Jesus from Egypt."

2. See Isaiah 60:3 and Psalm 68:29. "May the kings of Tarshish and of the isles render him tribute, may the kings of Sheba and Seba bring gifts! May all kings fall down before him, all nations serve him" (Ps 72:10–11).

3. Matthew 2:6, quoting Micah 5:2 and 2 Samuel 5:2.

4. No specific citation has been identified, so it is assumed that Matthew refers in 2:23 to a more general prophetic hope. Scholars have suggested on the one hand links to the Nazirite vow of consecration to God, and on the other, prophecies that God will bring a shoot (*nezer*) from the stump of Jesse (Isaiah 11:1). In this reading, God is making a new start with Jesus, of the line of David, bringing new life to a dead line and new hope for the future.

5. Matthew 2:15, quoting Hosea 11:1. The prophecy refers first to Israel and, at a deeper level, to the Messiah, the true Son of God.

6. Matthew 2:18; see Jeremiah 31:10–15.

7. Words of the Blessed Mother on June 13, 1917, according to Sr. Lucia, in "The Message of Fatima," Rosary Center, accessed February 8, 2018, http://www.rosary-center.org/fatimams.htm.

8. Thomas Merton, "Contemplation in a World of Action," from *Gethsemani Studies in Psychological and Religious Anthropology*, Second Edition, Restored and Corrected (Notre Dame, IN: University of Notre Dame Press, 1998).

6. Gaze with Prudence (Discovery in the Temple)

1. See, for example, Luke 4:43, John 9:4, Mark 8:31, and Luke 9:22.

2. John Paul II, General Audience (January 15, 1997), 2, 4.

3. Doug McManaman, "Prudence," LIFEISSUES.NET, January 2006. http://www.lifeissues.net/writers/mcm/mcm_56prudence1.html.

4. Fr. Alexis Lepicier, O.S.M., *Little Office of the Blessed Virgin Mary* (blog), accessed February 24, 2018, http://little-office-of-the-bvm.blogspot.it/2015/12/virgin-most-prudent-virtue-op-prudence.html.

5. *Flowers from the Garden of St. Francis for Every Day in the Year* (London: Burns and Oates, 1882), 33.

Conclusion

1. Deborah Savage, "The Nature of Woman in Relation to Man: Genesis 1 and Genesis 2 through the Lens of the Metaphysical Anthropology of St. Thomas. Aquinas," *Logos*, Winter 2014, 13.

2. Benedict XVI, "Way of the Cross at the Colosseum," Good Friday 2007, Fourth Station, http://www.vatican.va/news_services/liturgy/2007/documents/ns_lit_doc_20070406_via-crucis_en.html.

3. Thomas C. Fox, "Francis: 'The Gaze of Jesus Gives Us Dignity,'" *National Catholic Reporter*, September 21, 2013, https://www.ncronline.org/blogs/francis-chronicles/francis-gaze-jesus-gives-us-dignity. News report on the homily of Pope Francis on the Feast of St. Matthew.

Contributors

Alyssa Bormes is an author, speaker, and retreat leader who also teaches at the Chesterton Academy in Edina, Minnesota. She is the author of *The Catechism of Hockey* and has written for the *Catholic Spirit* and the *WINE: Women in the New Evangelization* blog. Bormes is the host of a weekly show, *Christian Witnesses in the Church,* on Radio Maria. You can find her at AlyssaBormes.com.

Sarah Christmyer is a Catholic author, Bible teacher, and speaker with a special love for lectio divina and journaling as ways to draw closer to Christ in scripture. She is codeveloper of The Great Adventure Catholic Bible study program and author or coauthor of many of its studies. Christmyer is an adjunct faculty member at St. Charles Borromeo Seminary in Philadelphia. She blogs at www.ComeIntotheWord.com.

Mary Healy is an international speaker and professor of scripture at Sacred Heart Major Seminary in Detroit. She is a general editor of the *Catholic Commentary on Sacred Scripture* and author of two of its volumes, *The Gospel of Mark* and *Hebrews.* Her other books include *Healing* and *Men and Women Are from Eden.* Healy is chair of the Doctrinal Commission of International Catholic Charismatic Renewal Services in Rome. She was appointed by Pope Francis as one of the first three women to serve on the Pontifical Biblical Commission.

Maria Morera Johnson is the author of *Super Girls and Halos* and the award-winning *My Badass Book of Saints.* She also contributed to *The Catholic Mom's Prayer Companion* and *Word by Word*. A *CatholicMom.com* contributor, Johnson retired in 2016 as a composition and literature professor and the director of English learning support at Georgia Piedmont Technical College. A native of Cuba, she and her husband, John, have three grown children and live near Mobile, Alabama. You can find her at MariaMJohnson.com.

Stephanie Landsem writes novels that bring the unknown women of the Bible to life. The Living Water series—*The Well*, *The Thief*, and *The Tomb*—presents biblically authentic stories of women who are transformed by encounters with Jesus. She lives in Minnesota with her husband and four children. You can find her at www.StephanieLandsem.com.

Elizabeth Lev is a Rome-based art historian who teaches Baroque art and architecture at Duquesne University's Italian campus and the history of Christian art in Rome for Christendom College. She has served as consultant on art and faith for the Vatican Museums and has published numerous articles and books including *The Tigress of Forlì*, *Roman Pilgrimage* (with George Weigel), and *A Body for Glory* (with Fr. Jose Granados). Her TED Talk on the Sistine Chapel has garnered more than 1.5 million views. Her website is www.ElizabethLev.com.

Joan Lewis is a columnist and EWTN special contributor for television and radio. She was named the network's first Rome bureau chief in 2005. She previously worked for the Vatican Information Service in the Holy See Press Office as the English language writer and editor and still hosts a program with Vatican Radio. Lewis was appointed a member of a number of Holy See delegations to United Nations conferences. In 2005, she was named Dame of the Order of St. Sylvester by Pope Benedict XVI for her work at the Holy See.

Deborah Savage is a member of the faculty at the St. Paul Seminary School of Divinity in St. Paul, Minnesota, where she teaches philosophy and theology and also directs the masters in pastoral ministry and religious education programs. Savage is the cofounder and director of the Siena Symposium for Women, Family, and Culture. Savage is a wife, a mother, an avid student of St. Thomas Aquinas, and a scholar of the work of Karol Wojtyla / St. John Paul II.

Katie Warner is a Catholic speaker, blogger, and author of the book *Head & Heart*. She is the manager of communication for Catholics Come Home and a correspondent for the *National Catholic Register*. Warner, a wife and mother, regularly shares resources for living a vibrant faith at home—including her popular prayer journal series—on her website, www.KatieWarner.com.

Carol Younger teaches graduate courses in school psychology and counseling and is active in adult faith formation in parishes. She is a senior fellow at the St. Paul Center for Biblical Theology. The author of *Retreat Companion for 33 Days to Morning Glory*, she presents at conferences and parishes on the unity of the Bible and the Salvation Story. The mother of three married children, Younger has seven grandchildren and two great-grandchildren.

Kelly Wahlquist is a Catholic author and speaker, and the founder of WINE: Women In the New Evangelization. She is the assistant director for the Archbishop Harry J. Flynn Catechetical Institute in the Archdiocese of St. Paul and Minneapolis.

Wahlquist is the author of *Created to Relate*, the editor of *Walk In Her Sandals*, and a contributing writer for WINE. Wahlquist leads women's pilgrimages through Italy and Ireland and travels around the country speaking on the New Evangelization. She lives in Minnesota with her husband, Andy, and their children.

catholicvineyard.com

Facebook: **WomenIntheNewEvangelization**

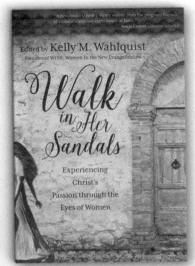